PRAIS

TWO PIECES of CLOTH

"I am moved beyond words... Joe Gold's *Two Pieces of Cloth* is an invaluable piece of not only one family's story, but emblematic of the story of the Holocaust. Joe has captured the first-hand feelings and experiences coupled with the historical background that contextualizes his family's story of resilience and survival. Joe's father, David Goldberger, is truly a heroic figure and leader—not just of his family, but of the Jewish people. The story of his survival is a testament to true faith and love. What kept him going during the darkness? Faith in God and love of family. The way Joe tells this story feels like first-person testimony—he has not only done justice and *kavod* to his parents and family's memory, but also provides the facts, photos, and stories that no denier can ever refute. Joe gives tremendous honour to his parents. *Kol Hakavod!*"

DR. WILLIAM RECANT, assistant executive vice president, American Joint Jewish Distribution Committee–International Development Program

"Another account of the Holocaust? Yes, indeed. *Two Pieces of Cloth* is an obvious labour of love, a generational testament to parents who survived the Shoah, and a treasure for our children and grandchildren. This is but one story of many that will remind the next generations of their past and help prepare them for the future. It is a powerful, authentic, and meaningful tribute to memory."

DR. ROBERT KRELL, professor emeritus, psychiatry, University of British Columbia; founding president, Vancouver Holocaust Education Centre

"Joe Gold shares the inspiring story of his family: a story of resilience, perseverance, faith, and hope in the face of indescribable evil. *Two Pieces of Cloth* is a significant contribution to the imperative of remembrance as the generations unfold and in the face of Holocaust denial."

J. ROLANDO MATALON, senior rabbi, Congregation B'nai Jeshurun, New York; founding co-director, Piyut North America

"A true treasure... *Two Pieces of Cloth* offers readers insight into the nature of human suffering and survival. Written with passion and precision."

DR. EVIE L. ROTSTEIN, RJE, senior education advisor, Hebrew Union College–Jewish Institute of Religion, New York School of Education

"In *Two Pieces of Cloth*, Joe Gold offers a vivid portrait of and tender tribute to his beloved parents, David and Aurelia Goldberger. Told in his parents' words, the story is bookended by Joe's perspective—first as a child getting a glimpse of his father's wartime experiences through the discovery of a book of concentration camp photographs hidden in his father's fabric store, and later as a seventy-two-year-old realizing his father's dream to write a book. Weaving together insights drawn from interviews and archival research, Joe does more than his stated goal of documenting the story for the benefit of his family; he offers a compelling intergenerational memoir of significance to those interested in the Holocaust and Vancouver history alike. David and Aurelia's story of unimaginable loss and unlikely survival—punctuated by luck, tenacity, faith, and an abiding love for family— makes their immense contributions to their adopted home in Canada all the more remarkable. We are all enriched by Joe's inheritance: to carry forward the memory of the Shoah for future generations."

NINA KRIEGER, executive director, Vancouver Holocaust Education Centre

"Joe Gold has absorbed the teaching of the Baal Shem Tov, the founder of Hasidism, that in remembrance lies the secret of redemption. Basing his book on various sources, including his father's oral testimony, he soberly conveys the history of his parents from their hometowns in Czechoslovakia through the horrors of the Holocaust, culminating in their eventual reunion and immigration to Canada. *Two Pieces of Cloth* is a sensitively written account of suffering and survival that allows the reader to understand the plight of European Jewry during World War II from the perspective of two individuals who emerged from the maelstrom without ever abandoning their humanity or their faith."

MENACHEM Z. ROSENSAFT, associate executive vice president, World Jewish Congress

TWO PIECES *of* CLOTH

One Family's Story of the Holocaust

JOE GOLD

PAGE TWO
BOOKS

Cataloguing in publication information is available
from Library and Archives Canada.
ISBN 978-1-989603-82-6 (paperback)
ISBN 978-1-989603-83-3 (ebook)

Page Two
www.pagetwo.com

Edited by Amanda Lewis
Copyedited by Shyla Seller
Proofread by Alison Strobel
Cover and interior design by Jennifer Lum
Cover photo and author headshot by Shira Gold
Interior maps by Eric Leinberger

www.twopiecesofcloth.com

Printed in Canada

To my beloved parents,
who survived the darkness of
the Holocaust and brought life to all of us.
They live in our hearts forever.

And to the many members of our family
who lost their lives in the Holocaust.
May their memory be for a blessing.

Ani Ma'amin Ba'Ameano Schaelemo.
I believe with a complete faith.
Never give up, never give up, you must have belief
in G-d and always be an optimist in spite of the odds.
Miracles can happen.

DAVID GOLDBERGER

Looking backward, we recall our ancestry.
Looking forward, we confront our destiny.
Looking backward, we reflect on our origins.
Looking forward, we choose our path.
Remembering that we are a tree of life, not letting go,
holding on, and holding to, we walk into an unknown,
beckoning future, with our past beside us.

RABBI HAROLD M. SCHULWEIS,
"Backwards and Forwards" (adapted)

MAP I

BEFORE WAR: 1939
Places of Interest[1]

100 miles

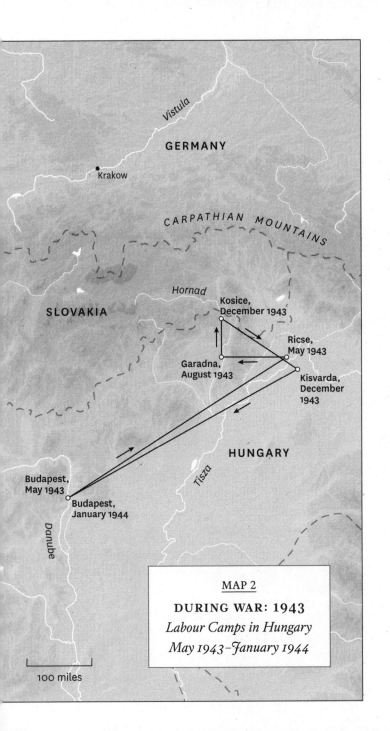

GERMANY

Vistula

Krakow

CARPATHIAN MOUNTAINS

Hornad

SLOVAKIA

Kosice,
December 1943

Ricse,
May 1943

Garadna,
August 1943

Kisvarda,
December
1943

HUNGARY

Tisza

Budapest,
May 1943

Budapest,
January 1944

Danube

MAP 2

DURING WAR: 1943
Labour Camps in Hungary
May 1943–January 1944

100 miles

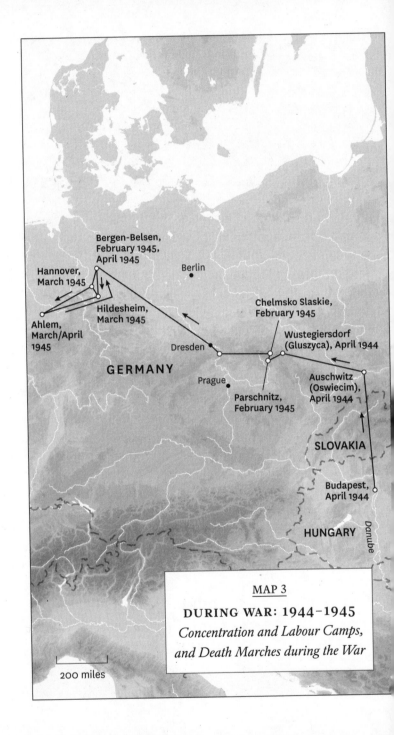

Bergen-Belsen,
February 1945,
April 1945

Berlin

Hannover,
March 1945

Chelmsko Slaskie,
February 1945

Hildesheim,
March 1945

Wustegiersdorf
(Gluszyca), April 1944

Ahlem,
March/April
1945

Dresden

Auschwitz
(Oswiecim),
April 1944

GERMANY

Prague

Parschnitz,
February 1945

SLOVAKIA

Budapest,
April 1944

HUNGARY

Danube

MAP 3

DURING WAR: 1944–1945
*Concentration and Labour Camps,
and Death Marches during the War*

200 miles

MAP 5
AFTER WAR: 1948

Vancouver,
June 1948

Montreal,
June 1948

Liverpool,
June 1948

Antwerp,
May
1948

Bratislava,
February
1948

*Atlantic
Ocean*

3,000 miles

Bergen-Belsen,
May 1945

Berlin

POLAND

Hannover, May 1945

Aller

Elbe

GERMANY

Prague,
May 1945

Vltava

CZECHOSLOVAKIA

Donau

Munich

Bratislava,
May 1945

Bratislava,
June 1945

AUSTRIA

Budapest,
May 1945

HUNGARY

Danube

MAP 4

AFTER WAR:
1945–1947

200 miles

CONTENTS

AUTHOR'S NOTE

IN THE fall of 2019, after many months of research, I began working on *Two Pieces of Cloth: One Family's Story of the Holocaust*. This book chronicles the history of my family from the end of World War I through June 1948, when we arrived in Canada. I wrote this book primarily for the benefit of my family, to give them a sense of where they came from.

I found it worked best to tell the story in the first person, in the words of my father and mother. I hope it is meaningful to the reader to experience the story in my parents' voices.

I pieced together their story using multiple sources. My father, David Goldberger, taped an interview with Dr. Robert Krell in 1984, as part of the Vancouver Holocaust Education Centre's Holocaust Documentation Project, and this recording, plus the conversations my brother Andrew and I had with our parents over the years, form the bulk of the narrative. I supported this information using documentation, such as marriage and birth certificates, reparation papers, as well as online resources from Yad Vashem and the United States Holocaust Memorial Museum.

I made my best effort to fill in the gaps using information I had at my disposal. Some facts may be inaccurate, as I am relying on memories of conversations which took place many years ago. Any factual errors are inadvertent and are my sole responsibility.

JOE

(1952)

ON SUNDAYS I would wake up early and spend the entire morning with my dad. This time together was very special to me, and I looked forward to it. We would go to my dad's fabric store on Granville Street in Vancouver, and I would help him. The store was extremely busy on Saturday, and certain chores needed to be finished on Sunday to have everything in place for Monday morning.

While my dad busied himself around the store, I worked "my job" at the thread and zipper displays. The thread display was beautiful: row upon row of bright colours, each with a number. Behind each spool was storage for another twelve spools. I would make sure that the colours were in their correct slot. Then I would open a cupboard under the display, where the reserve boxes of each colour were kept, and very carefully match the number on the box with the number on the display. It always amazed me that the black thread needed to be replenished most often.

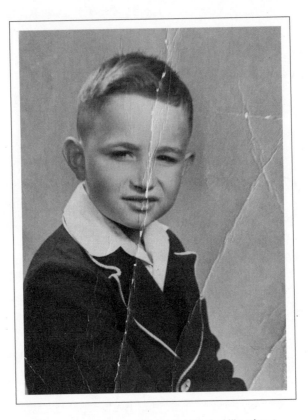

Me aged five in Vancouver. This is what I looked like when I found the book of photos in a bolt of fabric at my dad's fabric store.

After the threads were done, I would repeat the job with the zippers. There was an added challenge to this task, as I had to ensure that the zipper lengths all matched. It was time-consuming work and had to be done right. I wanted my dad to be pleased.

After my work was done and inspected, Dad always had a treat for me, usually a piece of chocolate or candy. I got to eat this in the back of the store, in an area that served both as an office and a storage room. My dad's desk was made of beautiful dark brown wood. On its top were slots for handling and organizing papers. There were drawers on both sides of the desk. The top drawer was a pullout shelf, which my dad and his staff used to eat their lunch. I got to use this shelf to eat my treat as well.

Across from the desk was an area used for storing large rolls of fabric. The ceiling was very high, and the fabric was piled on wooden shelves that went up about twenty feet. The shelves were perfect for me to climb. My favourite roll of fabric was up on the fourth row. I loved sticking my arm inside the large roll as far as I could to feel the softness of the wool and mohair. On the outside was dark purple, but on the inside was a golden and purple plaid.

On this particular day, when I stuck my hand inside the roll of fabric, I felt something hard. I grasped it and pulled it out. There, high on the shelf, I held a book with a tattered cover. I opened the book and saw pages of sad-looking children and long line-ups of men staring directly at me. As I flipped through the pages, I saw naked bodies that looked like skeletons. Some of these bodies were upright and some were lying down. On some pages, the skeletons were piled up one on top of the other. Some of the pages had people with bald heads and sad faces; they wore torn, striped pajamas. This book scared me. I heard my dad calling for me, and very quickly put the book back in the fabric roll where I had found it. It was time to go home for lunch.

I would look through the pages of this book a few more times during the next month, until the pictures were embedded in my brain.

One Sunday, my brother Andy came to the store with us. Andy was nine, four years older than me. I could hardly wait to show him the book that I had found in the roll. We went up together, and I reached inside the roll and pulled the book out. I gave it to him. Andy looked inside, shut it, and said, "This happened a long time ago, and we don't talk about it." With that, he climbed down with the book and left the room.

It would be another fifty-five years before I saw those pages of photographs again.

1

DAVID

(1914–1939)

M Y NAME is David Goldberger. My family and friends call me Deszer, or Deszy. I was born four-and-a-half months after the start of World War I, on December 7, 1914, in Benedikovce, Czechoslovakia.

I am the youngest of eight children: six boys and two girls. The two oldest were my half-brothers, Mark (Mayer) and Morris. Their last name was Liszovics. Mayer was eighteen years older than me. After the death of her first husband, my mother remarried and had twins, Sara and Mendel. After this there were Avraham (Pinchas), Yosef-Shalom (Joseph), Louisa, and me. Our last name was Goldberger.

My father, Heinrich (Chaim) Goldberger, was a schoolteacher, and my mother, Rozalia (Rosa) Friedman, looked after the household. I was told that my mother had a "good head for business."

Benedikovce was settled by Jews in the mid-eighteenth century. In 1880 they numbered 177. When I was born, it was a small city of approximately

5,000 people, of whom about ten percent were Jewish. Many of the Jews owned a factory that made alcohol. Ours was one of the larger families in town. With the shortages during the war and the size of our family, life was difficult. We were very poor.

In the winter of 1919, my mother slipped on an icy street and was hit by a horse and buggy. Her back was injured and she passed away a few months later. This made life even more difficult. At the age of five, I would sometimes go to different families in the neighbourhood to have dinner. I had a beautiful voice for my age, and would sing songs in exchange for a meal.

At this time, the war had ended. An independent Czechoslovakia was established on October 28, 1918, following the collapse of the Austro-Hungarian Empire. Prior to the war, the region consisted of Bohemia and Moravia, often called the Czech lands, in the west, and Slovakia, a part of Hungary, in the east.

Czechoslovakia's first president was Tomas Garrigue Masaryk, who headed a parliamentary democracy. The country concentrated seventy percent of the industry of the former Austro-Hungarian Empire, and its economy was among the strongest in the world.

My father decided it best that we pack all of our belongings and move to a larger city, where there were more opportunities for work. Our entire family moved to Bratislava, in the southwest of the country, on the banks of the Danube. Between 1867 and 1918, Bratislava (then Pressburg) was located within the borders of the Austro-Hungarian Empire. Following the war, the city became part of Czechoslovakia, and its name changed. It retained its role as the financial, cultural, and administrative centre for the Slovakian region. Until the middle of the nineteenth century, the majority of the city's inhabitants were German. After World War I, Slovaks and Czechs became the majority, with significant German, Hungarian, and Jewish minorities.

Bratislava had the largest Jewish community in Slovakia. It was a Jewish religious and political centre, and home to the renowned Pressburg Yeshiva, as well as the Zionist Organization of Slovakia. Some 15,000 Jews lived in the city, constituting around twelve percent of the population. Most of the Jewish population was either Orthodox or Neolog. Our family belonged to the Orthodox community.

My father got a job teaching in one of the Jewish high schools. He would teach at the school during the day, then tutor students in religious studies in the evening to earn extra money. While he worked, my two older sisters took care of the household. We had an aunt and uncle who lived in the city and helped us.

I began Grade 1 studies at a Jewish day school at the age of six. My oldest brother, Mayer, was a teacher there. He was also the master of the scouts youth group that I belonged to. Mayer was more than a brother to me. He was a father figure because of the special attention he gave me while our father worked day and night to try and make ends meet.

David and brother Mayer in Benedikovce. David is the first child on the left in the front row, the child without shoes. Mayer is the teacher in the middle of the second row.

"We were very poor... I would sometimes go to different families in the neighbourhood to have dinner... and would sing songs in exchange for a meal."

David's sisters Louisa (far left) and Sara (far right), and brothers Morris (standing) and Mayer (seated). This photo was taken in Cuba in 1938.

Mayer and Morris Liszovics were born in Munkacs, Czechoslovakia. Munkacs was also where David's brother Avraham lived prior to immigrating to Budapest in 1944.

Shortly after I started school, Mayer moved south, where the weather was warmer, to start a new life. He studied in Mexico City to become a doctor and eventually settled in Cuba.

My education consisted of eight years of studies—four years of elementary school and four years of middle school. I had general courses such as mathematics, reading, and writing, as well as Hebrew studies. I picked up many language skills and became fluent in Hungarian, Slovak, Czech, German, and Yiddish. After my Bar Mitzvah, I became active in the synagogue and had an opportunity to lead prayers. My older brothers Joseph and Avraham were also religious. I joined the Maccabi youth club and played soccer (centre forward) for recreation. We would play other Maccabi teams from many cities including Vienna, Budapest, Piestany, and Nitra.

During my last two years of middle school, I first encountered antisemitism. While we were walking to school, neighbourhood gangs would taunt us and threaten to beat us up. I was a fast runner, but one time, they caught me and beat me up. After that, I was given a pair of brass knuckles to help me defend myself. I used them on a few occasions, after which the gangs left us alone.

At age fourteen, I needed to start supporting myself, and decided that I wanted to become a businessman. In Europe at that time, you would apprentice in a business for three years without any pay. At the end of the three years, you would get a diploma, and after that you could get a job with wages. The textile and garment industry was mainly Jewish. There were many clothing and yard goods stores in the city.

I was lucky enough to find a job in a Jewish-owned textile business. The owner was able to give me room and board for the entire period of my apprenticeship. He was Orthodox and knew my father from the synagogue and the school. This textile company did a large business in both wholesale and retail, buying goods from mills and manufacturers throughout Europe and selling through a large retail store. They also sold to hundreds of small retail and general stores across Czechoslovakia.

Being an apprentice meant learning the business from the ground up. I started off doing janitorial work: washing the floors and windows, cleaning the washrooms. I ran errands for the owners and staff. Most of the sales staff in the store had worked on the floor for many years, especially the senior salesmen, who had experience anywhere from ten to thirty years. Ours was a well-regarded store, and we had many wealthy and well-known customers.

I worked my way up, and by the time I was fifteen, I worked in the stockroom. Here I sent and received shipments, learned how to create invoices for the bookkeepers, and reconciled the merchandise that came into the store. By the time I was sixteen, I assisted senior sales staff on the floor and replenished goods from the stockroom.

On one occasion, a very wealthy and important customer came into the store with his daughter, looking for wedding materials. They wanted something special. One by one, the senior sales staff offered fabrics to them. I watched as each of them was unable to make the sale. I had an idea, and asked the owner if I could try to please the customer. By this time, as I was spending time on the floor, I was wearing a suit and tie just like the sales staff. The owner gave me the authority to try, and introduced me to the customer.

I told them that we had just received a new shipment of goods, and that I wanted to show them something special. I went to the stockroom, where I knew every piece of fabric like the back of my hand. Knowing the colour that they were looking for, I took a roll of mauve taffeta from the shelf and wrapped it up in brown paper. I took the roll out to the floor, unwrapped it in front of them, and then rolled out a few yards for them to see. They loved the fact that something was brought out from the back specifically for them, and they said that it would be perfect. As a result of this sale, I was promoted to customer sales and service.

After three years, I received my diploma and was able to continue with the same company as an employee. I wanted to improve my salary and position in the company and worked long hours, sometimes twelve to fourteen hours a day, not the regular eight-hour days that everyone else worked.

When I had time, I would go to a business associ-
ation in the evenings. It was located in a house where
other apprentices from different vocations would
gather to discuss their businesses, read papers and
books, drink coffee, and enjoy each other's company.

I continued to work hard and learn the business.
Before long, I was helping the owner with the buying
and wholesale selling. I worked my way up to general manager and was given a share position in the
company. I would be responsible for setting up the
store displays, ad campaigns, and special sales events.
Later, I would travel by train to major cities and meet
with the jobbers and manufacturers, buying large
amounts of fabric. I then took on the regional sales
management for the company's wholesale business.
I would travel by train, a few times a year, to many
smaller cities and towns, offering our line of goods to
the yard goods stores and general stores throughout
the countryside.

Life was good. I was making a very good living and
enjoyed what I was doing. I made many acquaintances
and friends all over the country on my sales calls. For
the first time in my life, I could afford to buy myself
new shoes and suits. I loved style, and would have
my suits made to measure, complete with vests. In
my limited spare time, I would go to events that were
sponsored by the Mizrachi movement, a religious
Zionist organization that was founded in 1902. B'nei
Akiva, which was founded in 1929, is the youth movement that was associated with Mizrachi. There were

a great many organizations that one could attend at that time. I would go to synagogue on Shabbat and the Jewish holidays. I loved music, especially the synagogue prayers sung by the chazzan. Bratislava was beautiful and a wonderful place to live.

Then, in 1938, when I was twenty-four, things started to change.

Tomas Garrigue Masaryk was the president of Czechoslovakia from 1919 to 1935. He fought antisemitism and was a staunch sympathizer of the Zionist movement and pleaded for the creation of a Jewish state. Under his leadership, Jewish people were able to conduct their lives freely.

When Masaryk resigned from his post of president in 1935 due to illness, and at the age of eighty-five, he was replaced by Edvard Benes. Benes was a politician and statesman who was president of Czechoslovakia from 1935 to 1938 and again from 1945 to 1948. He resigned after the Munich Agreement and subsequent German occupation of Czechoslovakia in 1938, which brought his government into exile in the United Kingdom. Before his time as president, from 1918 to 1935, he was the minister of foreign affairs.

Benes had been groomed by Masaryk to become his successor. He left his post of foreign minister and continued the liberal internal policy of Masaryk towards the Jewish people in Czechoslovakia as well as supporting the Jewish national home in Palestine. It was around this time that the German inhabitants of the Czech border areas called the Sudetenland began calling for autonomy—they wanted to be German again.

In September 1938, Germany, Britain, France, and Italy signed the Munich Agreement, giving Adolf Hitler the right to invade and claim Czechoslovakia's border areas, despite the fact that France had a treaty with Czechoslovakia promising to help in the event of military aggression. On March 15, 1939, Hitler's army invaded Czechoslovakia. Czechoslovakia, only twenty years old, was partitioned into three regions. Bohemia and Moravia (Sudeten region) were annexed and became the protectorate of the Third Reich. The fascist autonomous state of Slovakia, including Bratislava, was formed under the presidency of Dr. Jozef Tiso, a former priest, and Prime Minister Vojtech Tuka. As a result of the 1938 Munich Agreement, the eastern part of the country (northern Transylvania), inhabited by Hungarian-speaking people, was given to Hungary in August 1940.

Jozef Tiso had been imprisoned many years earlier for activities against the democratic government of Czechoslovakia. His wife, living alone, was treated extremely well by the Jewish community, as she was in need of welfare. She even frequented our fabric store and was given fabrics for clothing. Even so, the situation for Jews worsened under Tiso. The Jews of Bratislava were the first Slovakian Jews to endure humiliations, persecutions, and financial restrictions.

I was close to twenty-six years old by this time and well established as general manager of the company.

My father, David Goldberger, was always a stylish dresser. Here he is in 1939 at age twenty-five, already a successful textile salesman and manager of a business called Kaiser Textiles.

Every day there would be a full page of new laws for the Jewish people in the newspaper. These new laws were aimed at limiting the freedom of Jews in all German-controlled territories and Slovakia, and isolating them from the non-Jewish population, whom were now called "Aryan."

Lieutenant Colonel Adolf Eichmann, an official within Hitler's paramilitary organization, the SS, had been sent to Bratislava. He coauthored a plan with Tiso and other Ludak politicians to deport foreign Jews. The Ludak were members of a far-right political party with a Catholic fundamentalist and authoritarian ideology. They were against liberalism and wanted Slovak autonomy. I saw Eichmann as his motorcade entered Bratislava on the bridge. I also saw thousands of Jewish refugees who were being deported back to countries such as Poland that the Nazis had seized. These refugees included young children, the elderly, and pregnant women. They were on foot and had nothing except for whatever personal belongings they could carry.

At the end of 1939, the licences of most of the Jewish doctors and lawyers were revoked by the government of Slovakia, and many Jewish public officials were fired. Hundreds of families were forced to hurriedly abandon their apartments in central areas of the city—they had to crowd together in the Jewish quarter in bad conditions. Their confiscated property was handed over to state and party supporters. Jewish students were expelled from public schools. In 1941, the authorities increased their efforts to divest Jews of their property.

One of my wholesale customers, Josef Birnbaum, owned a general store in the small town of Spisske Vlachy, 239 miles from Bratislava. The store had all kinds of household merchandise, clothing, shoes, and fabrics. Above the store was his family home, where he lived with his wife and five daughters. It was there I met Aurelia.

2

AURELIA

(1915-1941)

MY NAME is Aurelia Birnbaum. My family calls me Aranka. I was born on September 17, 1915, in Spisske Vlachy, eastern Czechoslovakia. I was the second oldest of five girls: Elizabeth (1913), Dorothy (1917), Gisella (1920), and Magda (1922).

My mother's name was Malka Riff. She was born in Svidnik, Czechoslovakia, in 1892, the eldest of ten children born to Bernard and Regina Riff. Svidnik was about sixty miles from Spisske Vlachy. My mother died at age thirty, after Magda was born. I was eight years old. My mother's sister Eva came to Spisske Vlachy and married my father, Josef Birnbaum, in 1923. She was only nineteen years old and looked after all of us. She was a wonderful stepmother and aunt to us, and we loved her very much.

My father was born on April 14, 1888, in Spisske Podhradie, about five miles from Spisske Vlachy. He was one of seven children born to Moshe and Sara Birnbaum. He moved to Spisske Vlachy in his early twenties and had his own place of business from 1912 until 1942.

Spisske Vlachy is in the Spis region, administered as part of the Kosice region, Kosice being the largest city, about thirty-five miles away. Our town is situated just north of the Hornad River, near its confluence with the Margencanka stream. It is a mountainous area with a temperate climate. The area south of the town has meadows and fertile land with many small lakes. The famous ruins of the Spis Castle are nearby. It was a beautiful area to grow up in.

My father's textile and general store was one of the businesses that served the needs of our town. He was very well known, and there were many articles about him in the local newspaper. His father, who ran a general store that specialized in shoes, clothing, and fabrics, in a neighbouring town, had helped him establish the business. Salesmen from all over the country would frequent my father's store to sell their wares. My older sister and I helped our father in the store after school and on weekends.

We had a house above the store and a garden in the back. Here we planted and harvested vegetables, had apple and plum trees, and had a yard to play in. We were all taught how to sew and cook. When we were teenagers, we would sew most of our own clothes.

Our country was surrounded by Hungary, Austria, Poland, and Ukraine. We had joined together with the First Czechoslovak Republic in 1918. Residents of my area mainly spoke Slovakian and Hungarian. Our dialect was similar to that of Polish and Russian, and we

Aurelia Birnbaum and her sisters. She was the second oldest of five girls, pictured left to right: Elizabeth, Aurelia, Dorothy, Gisella, and Magda.

had many words that were the same in Hungarian. In school I also learned how to speak Czech and German.

Due to our central location and complex history, many of our Slovak dishes also exist in surrounding countries. But we always added our own special twist to our cooking. Our main meals used a lot of meat, chicken, potatoes, and dumplings. Delicious bread from the bakery was a big staple in our household. Our favourite local dishes to cook were potato dumplings stuffed with cheese; cabbage soup with beef and knedle; goulash soup with beef, onions, potatoes, peppers, tomatoes, and garlic; schnitzel with fried potatoes; potato pancakes—which were crunchy on the outside but gooey and soft on the inside—and crepes called "palacinky" filled with apricot or strawberry jam and sprinkled with powdered sugar and cinnamon. We also cooked many Hungarian dishes such as chicken paprikash, potato casserole, green pea soup with beef, and stuffed cabbage with minced beef. Another favourite dish was dumplings served with grated farmer cheese and breadcrumbs browned in butter. Our baking favourites were babka cakes with cinnamon, chocolate, or walnuts, and a variety of cheesecakes. Our favourite dessert was fruit compote.

We mostly walked or rode bicycles. We would ride the railway for trips to nearby towns. The railway was connected to my grandparents' town, Spisske Podhradie, only a few miles away.

Our family celebrated all of the Jewish holidays, and my sisters and I went to the local public school as well as Jewish studies after school and on Sundays. My favourite activity other than school was gymnastics. I belonged to a group called Young Israel and the Bet Yaakov girls' movement, where I had many friends.

I attended the middle grade and high schools in our town. For the year after high school (which was called "gymnasium") I stayed with my grandparents in Spisske Podhradie, which had the best school for ongoing studies in the area. I wanted to become a nurse and took courses related to nursing. On the weekends, I would go back to my parents' home and help out in my father's store. By this time, my older sister, Elizabeth, had married Aharon (Erno) Birnbaum, a cousin of ours. Elizabeth moved to Putnok, Hungary, where Aharon's family all lived and had a large general store. In 1938, the year they married, they had a son named Egon. My younger sister, Dorothy (Dodke), married Carl Roth in 1940, who was also from our town.

A man from Bratislava, David Goldberger, came to our store every season with his samples of merchandise. He would generally come by train from Kosice. Quite often, my father would invite him to stay at our home for dinner. I thought he was very handsome and well dressed, a real gentleman.

One day in the spring of 1941, when David visited our home, my father had a big discussion with him about what was going on in the country and about his future. We were hearing news about new laws and problems for the Jewish communities in the larger cities. My father was involved with the Keren Kayemeth LeIsrael—collecting the blue boxes in our community—and had first-hand knowledge of Israel (Palestine), and of many young people who were leaving Europe for Israel. He thought it would be best if David and I married. If not now, when? He also thought we should live as a married couple during what might become a very difficult time. The very next day, David Goldberger proposed to me.

We were married on June 17, 1941, in the spa town of Piestany, with our families present.

I was so very excited about my future with David. It was a lovely time.

My mother, Aurelia, in 1939. She was twenty-four, and in two years would marry my father, David Goldberger.

3

DAVID

(1941–1945)

I HAD MUCH family in the surrounding areas of Bratislava. Through my travels, I made many friends there, too. My brother Yosef-Shalom (Joseph), who was a teacher, together with his wife Sara, son Moshe Tov-Yehia, and daughter Renate, lived in a neighbourhood in Bratislava. Our good friend Eugen Marmorshtein from Nitra, whose father was a rabbi of the Neolog community, was one of the witnesses at my wedding in Piestany. Another of my best friends was Heinrich Hoffman, from Piestany. He was the other witness at our wedding who signed our ketubah (marriage certificate).

Aranka and I were married in a large and beautiful Orthodox synagogue with 400 seats, which had been built in 1904. Rabbi Josef Unger officiated. Rabbi Unger came from a long line of rabbis who served in Piestany and Nitra. My brother Yosef-Shalom studied at yeshiva with a relative of Rabbi Unger.

Piestany is only an hour from Bratislava, and I was fortunate to have visited there often. It was famous as a health and vacation town, and people visited from all over the country, and from other countries too. There were beautiful hotels and natural spring baths, and there was much lively cultural activity. We had a lovely wedding and honeymoon. Looking back, it was all too short, as a different reality awaited us soon thereafter.

We lived in a small apartment in a Jewish neighbourhood, walking distance to the main synagogue at Sklar 5, in Bratislava. I returned to my place of business, only to find out that it was being Aryanized. This meant that a German businessman was given majority control of our business. This particular person had many different kinds of businesses, of which ours was the only textile company. Because of this, he obtained permission to employ Jews and paid a fee for the licence to do so. This licence had to be renewed periodically. My expertise as general manager of the company was necessary for him, and I continued on with my normal activities under very stressful circumstances.

The local authorities continued to impose anti-Jewish measures. Jews were ordered to wear a yellow band around their left arm, which led to many attacks. To systematize antisemitic legislation, Slovak legislators passed the Jewish Code on September 9, 1941: 270 anti-Jewish articles, largely focused on removing Jews from the economy. Slovak propaganda boasted that this Jewish Code was the strictest set of anti-Jewish laws in Europe. The president, however, could issue exemptions protecting individual Jews from the law. Employed Jews were initially exempt from some of the code's requirements, such as wearing the yellow band. At the time, my wife and I had this kind of status.

One of the requirements of the new legislation was to hand in any insurance policies. Aranka was a beneficiary of a life insurance policy that her father had put in place many years prior for the benefit of his two eldest daughters, should anything happen to him. I was required to hand this policy in to the authorities at the local bank. I did so. Failure to do this could result in severe punishment, had the document been found.

In November 1941, a second Aryanization law was passed, mandating the expropriation of Jewish property and the dismissal of Jewish employees. Ten thousand Jewish businesses were liquidated and the remainder—about 2,300—were Aryanized. I was kept on, but an Aryan was hired to learn the business from me.

The Aryanization and liquidation of businesses was nearly complete by January 1942, resulting in unemployment for 64,000 of the 89,000 Slovak Jews. Jewish impoverishment created a pressing social problem for the Slovak government, which it "solved" in the spring of 1942 by deporting the Jews who had been forced into unemployment.

Despite the government's belief that the Slovak Republic would benefit from Aryanization, it was an immense financial loss to the country's economy. The state failed to raise substantial funds from the sale of Jewish property and businesses, and most of its gains came from the confiscation of Jewish-owned bank accounts and financial securities. The main beneficiaries of Aryanization were members of Slovak fascist political parties and paramilitary groups, who were eager to acquire Jewish property but had little interest (or expertise) in running Jewish businesses. During Slovakia's existence, the government gained 1.1 billion korunas from Aryanization and spent 900–950 million korunas on enforcing anti-Jewish measures. In 1942, it paid the German government an additional 300 million korunas for the deportation of 58,000 Jews. Except for Croatia, Slovakia was the only country that paid to deport its Jewish population.

At the Wannsee Conference in January 1942, Reinhard Heydrich said that implementing the Final Solution in Slovakia would not be very difficult. Jozef Tiso most likely helped initiate the deportations. In fact, Tiso presented deportation proposals to the government on March 3, 1942.

The Slovaks agreed to pay 500 Reichsmarks per Jew deported (supposedly to cover the cost of resettlement and retraining), and an additional fee to the Deutsche Reichsbahn for transportation. The Germans promised in exchange that the Jews would never return, and that Slovakia could keep all the confiscated property.

In Spisske Vlachy, our family's business and home were confiscated. Single women and girls were rounded up and sent to detention holding centres in

Poprad. On March 25, 1942, the first train departed from Poprad transit camp for Auschwitz, with 1,000 unmarried Jewish women between the ages of sixteen and forty-five, in cattle cars. Some guards and local officials accepted bribes to keep Jews off the transports. Aranka's father Josef did his best to save his youngest daughters from deportation, but on April 2, 1942, Aranka's sisters Gisella (Gisi) and Magda were deported from Poprad to Auschwitz.

SS leader Heydrich visited Bratislava on April 10, and he and Prime Minister Vojtech Tuka agreed that further deportations would target whole families and eventually remove all Jews from Slovakia.

Members of the Hlinka Guard were in charge of rounding up the Jews, guarding transit centres, and eventually loading them into overcrowded cattle cars for deportation. The Hlinka guardsmen also chased and assaulted Jews in the streets and stole their last possessions.

The family transports began on April 11, 1942. Transports went to Auschwitz after mid-June, where a minority of the victims were selected for labour, and the remainder were killed in the gas chambers. This occurred for eight transports, the last of which arrived on October 21, 1942. These and other transports included Aranka's parents and sister Dorothy, together with her husband. They also included my father, and my brother Yosef-Shalom with his wife and children. They all perished except for Magda, who was selected for work and was liberated at the end of the war.

In the spring of 1942, several thousand Jews fled to Hungary, aided by Rabbi Shmuel Dovid Ungar and the youth movements. Most of those who were successful in crossing the border bribed the guards to let them through or paid smugglers. Many others were arrested at the border and immediately deported. Widespread resistance by the Working Group (an underground organization) opposed the deportations, which drove the Hlinka Guard to forcibly round up Jews to fill transports and deport Jews who had been promised immunity to labour camps.

It was time for us to make a plan. I was certain that once the new owner of our business decided that he no longer needed me, we would be rounded up and deported. I saw this happen with many other businesses and friends. I needed to find a person who would be able to provide us with false papers and arrange for our safe passage to Budapest.

Hungary was still a safe place for us, as it had sided with Germany. Despite losses and hardships caused by anti-Jewish legislation, the majority of Hungary's Jewish community at this time lived in relative security. We would need to travel from Bratislava, through the border region, to the area that was given to Hungary by the Germans, through a no man's land, and into Hungary proper. I needed someone who knew people that could help us in each of these areas. The total distance from Bratislava to Budapest is 124 miles.

Before World War II, approximately 200,000 Jews lived in Budapest, making it the centre of Hungarian

Jewish cultural life. In the late 1930s and early 1940s, Budapest was a safe haven for Jewish refugees. Before the war some 5,000 refugees, primarily from Germany and Austria, arrived in Budapest. With the beginning of the deportations of Jews from Slovakia in March 1942, as many as 8,000 Slovak Jewish refugees also settled in Budapest.

Our plan to escape to Budapest materialized in September 1942. Once I had all the identification documents and other necessary border papers in place from one source, and arrangements in place for safe passage from another source, I came home from work one evening and told Aranka that we were going to leave the next day. The borders of both Hungary and Slovakia were patrolled by the gendarme, the border police. If we were caught without proper identification, they would immediately send us to jail.

In order not to cause suspicion, we packed only one small suitcase, with very little in the way of personal belongings. For the same reason, we took little cash with us, only what we needed for train tickets and food. Our plan was to travel by train to a small village on the border of Slovakia. We were to stay there overnight and had arranged to be picked up the next morning by two men who would guide us by foot through the border area (no man's land) to the Hungarian side, where we would spend the evening. Early the next morning, we would be picked up by a man with a horse and buggy who was to take us to the station where we would then take the train to Budapest.

We were greeted at the railroad station on the Slovak border, as planned, by a woman who ran a small inn. She had been paid well to give us a meal and a room for the evening. She was very kind and served us a meal of milk and cheese with bread. The next day we began to worry, as the whole morning went by and we had not seen her. As she was not a young person, we thought that perhaps something happened to her. We didn't see her the whole afternoon. What had happened? Then, all of a sudden, she came back at dinnertime, around six in the evening. We were so relieved to see her, as the plan called for the two men to come later that evening between eight and ten to take us over to the Hungarian side.

The two men finally came after ten o'clock. It was completely dark outside as we followed them out of the town. All of a sudden, we heard barking dogs and men's voices. This scared us, and we could feel our hearts beating quickly. Would the border police pick us up for being out late at night walking across the border?

After one hour we made it safely and finally arrived at their home on the Hungarian side. We were given a meal and a room for a short rest, as we needed to be up at three in the morning to prepare ourselves to be picked up. Shortly thereafter, two men arrived, a father and a son, together with a horse and buggy. Right away, they started to tell us that they would not take us to the station unless they were paid more money. They argued that they were not paid enough and that the risk was too great for them. I knew that they were paid a lot of money (a few thousand korunas) as part of the arrangement. We were in big trouble, as we only carried enough money to pay for our train tickets, approximately ten dollars. We could not offer them anything more. It would have been very dangerous to carry large sums of cash if we were caught. We therefore only took what was needed.

After a lot of arguing, I finally asked if they were going to take us or not. If we didn't leave soon, we would miss the train. I guess they realized that we really did not have any more money, and they decided to take us to the station as arranged. We got to the station twenty minutes before the train was to arrive. I had never been to this station before and was unsure of the procedures needed to purchase a ticket. Although I spoke Hungarian, the local dialects were different than those I knew, and I needed to present myself as a local in case our identification papers were checked.

I went to the cashier in the ticket booth and noticed that the currency was the Hungarian pengo. I asked the man for two tickets to Budapest, gave him the pengos that were worth about ten dollars, and he gave me some change. As I waited for the tickets, I noticed that there were gendarmes all over the station. They wore a distinctive feather in their cap, and were known to be very antisemitic and very tough.

Aranka was waiting for me on the platform. She spoke Hungarian with a different dialect. She was also pregnant at this time. I saw the policeman approaching her and quickly went to her with the tickets. The gendarme said that he wanted to see our identification. I showed him the papers and he asked me questions. I had prepared myself in case this should happen. He wanted to know where we were going and where we had come from. I told him that we were going to Budapest for only a couple of days and gave him the name of the small town in Hungary that we lived in as per our false papers. At that moment the train arrived and we were given back our papers. We were so relieved once we were in our seats and on the train to Budapest.

Then the reality sunk in. Here we were, safely on the train, yet we had no money, didn't know anyone in Budapest, and had nowhere to stay once we arrived. Sitting near us were a few couples and a single man. I could tell that this well-dressed young man was Jewish and for some reason, I was compelled to go over and talk to him. Something within me said that God had sent him to me, that he could help us. So, very carefully, not knowing who the other people were, I went over and introduced myself.

He was from a town that was at one time in Czechoslovakia and was now part of the land given back to Hungary by Hitler. His last name was Kastner. I very quietly told him that we lived in Bratislava and were on our way to Budapest. I explained our dire circumstance to him. He said to me, "Don't worry my friend, I will look after you."

He was engaged, and his fiancée lived in Budapest. He travelled to Budapest every few days. She was waiting at the train station for him. He greeted her and introduced us. The first thing they said to us was that we needed to have a place to stay. They took us to a beautiful, first-class hotel and registered us at the front desk for a room. He explained that the police detectives went to the cheaper hotels on a daily basis looking for anyone with false papers.

They told us that they wanted to take us out to a nice restaurant that had some entertainment where we could enjoy ourselves a little bit after such a difficult journey. We were hesitant, but they insisted.

We were taken to our room to get settled and freshen up. An hour later, they came to pick us up. They had brought a fresh shirt for me and a fresh blouse for Aranka. We had a lovely time with them. We all went back to the hotel together and we thanked them very much for all their kindness. He offered me some money, which I did not want to take; however, once more he insisted.

I explained to him that Aranka had a sister and brother-in-law who lived in Putnok, and that they would be able to help us once we were able to contact them. I sent them a telegram from the hotel letting them know that we had safely arrived in Budapest. I assessed what we had left: only enough for the next day, approximately one hundred pengos. I was certain that help would arrive shortly. It had to.

Putnok was a town in northern Hungary, 135 miles from Budapest, with a population of 7,000. This is where Aranka's older sister Elizabeth (Birji) and Aharon Birnbaum lived. Aharon was also a cousin to Aranka. We had been in touch earlier to tell them that we were making a plan to get out of Slovakia and hopefully travel to Budapest. Of course, we didn't know when that would happen, so we told them that we would send a telegram once we had arrived, if we did arrive. I had wired money to them so that they could purchase clothing and other personal items that we would need. I also wired money separately for them to hold for us so that we could afford to rent a room in an apartment to get started.

We thanked the Kastners so much for all the help they had given us and said goodbye. We went to sleep until suddenly, around six o'clock in the morning, there was a knock on the door. We were frightened. Was it the police? No, we were very lucky. It was a telegram from Aranka's sister saying that her brother-in-law, Albert (Shani), would be arriving at the hotel at seven-thirty to see us.

Albert arrived with food and two large suitcases full of clothing for both of us. He explained that Aharon, our brother-in-law, could not come, as he had been drafted by the authorities the day before to serve in the Hungarian army. Jewish men of military age were forced to join.

We stayed with Albert for a week while he helped find us a place to live. It was difficult, because very few were willing to risk renting to people who were in the country illegally. Finally, we found an apartment with two bedrooms. In the other room lived a young married couple in the same situation as we were. The man, named Frankel, found work as a labourer in a furniture factory. He spoke Hungarian very well and in Slovakia had worked as a salesman in a high-end menswear store. His wife was a dressmaker and worked as a seamstress from the apartment. We became very friendly with them. Aranka knew how to sew very well and the two of them worked together. They helped Frankel's wife's customers buy fabrics, and sewed dresses and coats for them.

One of the ladies for whom they made custom clothes came from a very wealthy family in Budapest. They owned several well-known fabric and notion stores in Budapest, Koray Textiles. They sold retail and wholesale. Frankel's wife knew that I wanted to work, and she knew from Aranka that I had worked in the fabric business in Bratislava. She spoke to the wealthy customer, and asked if there might be some work for me. A few days later, she came back to the apartment to try on a dress and told me that she had spoken to her husband and that he would like to meet me.

I walked into his office the next day. He was a very tall gentleman. After talking with me, he offered me a job. But first I needed to change my name to a Hungarian name, which he gave me. There was a Hungarian law mandating that only a certain percentage of a business's employees could be Jewish. Of the one hundred employees in his business, he had already met the limit of five percent. So, I took on the new name, was introduced to the rest of the staff, and started to work with the company. My salary was not very high, but together with Aranka's dressmaking and some help from Elizabeth and Albert, we made ends meet.

A while later, Frankel was able to find a much better job, but it was far away from the apartment. Frankel and his wife moved out to be closer to work, and we also decided to move so that I could be within walking distance of the store and not have to pay for the bus twice daily, as we had to save every penny I made. By this time, Aranka was not able to work any longer as she was in her last month of pregnancy.

One morning, I went to the synagogue. There was a small cafeteria next door, and I would always bring home two little buns with butter and a coffee for Aranka. When I got to our floor in the building, there were two men waiting. Aranka was already dressed. They looked at me and refused to believe that I was Aranka's husband. They said that it was impossible for us to be married, as she was definitely not Jewish, because she did not look Jewish. They accused me of lying, even though I showed them the bag with breakfast for my wife. They then took out identification from their jackets' inside pockets, and showed me that they were detectives. They took us to the police station.

We later learned that authorities had stopped a man from Bratislava on the train to Hungary as he was boarding. They searched his baggage and found a pile of torn paper, as well as a pile of money. They arrested him. When they reassembled the scraps of paper, they found the names and addresses of individuals for whom he had provided false identification, and who had come into Hungary. He had torn the papers into small pieces once he boarded, as he had a feeling that he might be searched later.

This was the man I had hired to make new identification and arrange for our passage to Budapest. Once settled in our apartment, I had wired my address to him as I, along with many others, had given him money to bring to us at a later date. This was part of the plan. That's why the detectives had been at our door. Aranka and I were taken back to our place and forced to gather our belongings.

There was an area in the old city of Pest, called the Rumbach area, that was set up as a ghetto. It was the part of the city where the authorities gathered those who were in the country illegally. We told our cousin and sister-in-law what had happened to us. They immediately hired a lawyer and worked very hard to have Aranka moved into the main hospital of Budapest. They had to guarantee to the hospital that they would pay all costs. They also agreed to sponsor and look after both Aranka and the baby, which would allow them to stay in the country. This was in early May 1943. We were then separated for over eight months.

All of the Jewish male illegals from ages eighteen to forty-five, married and single, were sent away to form labour battalions. I was sent to an area near

Ricse, a small town in Zemplen county, in northern Hungary. Ricse was 186 miles from Budapest. Prior to this time, in 1941, the young Jews of Ricse were mobilized for forced labour; only a few survived. Here we were separated into labour battalions and sent to do all kinds of work in the northern area of the country.

There were many men from Bratislava in this battalion that I previously knew as business associates and friends. Besides illegals, there were also communist sympathizers in the labour camp. While in a camp near the small town of Garadna, fifty-eight miles from Ricse, I finally got word from Budapest that my wife had given birth to our child, a boy. Special arrangements were made whereby an army official would take me back to Budapest to see my little boy. I was so happy to hear this news. We were to leave together at four o'clock in the afternoon. That same afternoon, just before I was to leave for Budapest, we got word that all of the labour camps in the area had to pack up. We were all going to be taken to a gathering place outside the city of Kosice (Hungarian: Kassa) where the military had a large base.

The next morning we left for Kosice, which was twenty-three miles away. We arrived early in the morning. All together, with our camp and several others, there were about 1,500 men. Many of them I recognized from my home city of Bratislava. We were told that we were all being sent to the front lines in Russia to dig trenches for the army. We had been waiting at the holding area from early morning. It was

December 15, 1943. There was ice on the ground and it was snowing. We had been waiting outside from six-thirty in the morning until one o'clock in the afternoon without any food or water.

Large flatbed trucks arrived half an hour later and the process began. They started calling out names of the individuals that had been on registry lists from the various camps. Every time fifty or sixty names had been called, those men and boys were put onto a truck, and they left for the front. Not a single one of these men made it back. They were all killed on the Russian front. I know this because there were probably 100 to 120 names called out that I recognized, friends of mine from Bratislava, whom I never saw again after the war.

After all the names had been called, there were only two people left standing: me, and another man who was hard of hearing. A large Hungarian officer came up to us. He was very angry and started yelling at us in Hungarian, saying that if our names were found to be on the list that we would be shot immediately. Together with two other soldiers we followed him into an interrogation room. There were pictures on the wall, perhaps pictures of spies who had been caught. I was so scared and thought that this was going to be the last few minutes of my life, that I was going to be shot. They went through every name on the list again, and thank God, our names were not there.

We spent the night in jail together. The next day, we were sent sixty-six miles to Kisvarda, in the

Northern Great Plain region of eastern Hungary near the border of Slovakia and Ukraine. Prior to World War II, Kisvarda had a large Jewish community, about thirty percent of the town's population. They were confined to a ghetto in 1944, and then deported to Auschwitz. A small community was re-established after the war, but almost no Jews are left in Kisvarda today. The former synagogue, which remains one of the most imposing structures in Kisvarda, is now a local history museum known as the Retkozi Muzeum.

Kisvarda is on the main railway line from Budapest to Ukraine. I was put in a labour battalion that mainly worked on repairing the railway line.

MEANWHILE, ARANKA, together with our son, had been staying with her sister and brother-in-law in Budapest, all the while working with the authorities to release me from the labour camps. Our brother-in-law Aharon had returned safely from his duty with the Hungarian army.

Having spent a great deal of money, they were able to arrange for me to come back to Budapest under the condition that I would go to the immigration office on either the first or fifteenth of each month and register myself. This process would grant me a monthly visa to stay in the country.

I returned to Budapest and was able to see my wife and meet my son Andreus (Andrew, Moshe) for the first time. He was named after Aranka's grandfather, Moshe Birnbaum. The wonderful doctor who

My parents with Andrew in their first family photo, 1943.
This was the first time David saw Andrew. My mother and
brother were in Budapest, and my father was put in a forced
labour battalion in eastern Hungary, mainly repairing the
railroad line.

delivered our son at the hospital was named Andrew. Our son was born in the month of May, in 1943, a blessing from God amidst very frightening times.

Despite the loss of tens of thousands, and hardship caused by anti-Jewish legislation, the majority of Hungary's Jewish community lived in relative security until March 1944. In the meantime, in much of occupied Europe, the Holocaust was already in full swing. SS mobile extermination units swept through the eastern territories, death camps and forced labour camps were operating, and Jewish communities were destroyed one after the other. Between 1942 and 1944, Prime Minister Miklos Kallay's conservative government, while passing a number of anti-Jewish laws and making extremist antisemitic statements, still rejected German demands to deport Hungarian Jews.

The relative sense of security evaporated on March 19, 1944, when German troops occupied Hungary. The occupation was motivated primarily by the fact that Berlin got wind of cease-fire talks between Hungary and the Allies, and Hitler wanted to prevent Hungary from following the example of Italy and deserting the war effort. Moreover, Germany planned to exploit the Hungarian economy more effectively than before to cover the increasing costs of the war. The "Jewish question" played but a secondary role in the country's occupation.

The German army was accompanied by a special unit (Sondereinsatzkommando—SEK) with orders to "dejewify" the country. The SEK was placed under the command of SS-Lieutenant Colonel Adolf Eichmann, chief of the Reich Security Head Office, which was responsible for Jewish deportations across Europe. The SEK had no more than twenty officers and a force of over one hundred (including drivers, guards, and secretaries). It was obvious that on its own, without the cooperation of the Hungarian authorities, the unit could not organize the collection of 760,000–780,000 Jews scattered all over the country within an area of 105,000 square miles.

Under German pressure, a few days following the occupation in March 1944, Regent Miklos Horthy appointed a collaborating government ready to serve Nazi interests. The Hungarian Interior Ministry and its gendarmerie, both of whose members had close links to the Arrow Cross, cooperated with the Germans with unexpected zeal. The Arrow Cross Party was a far-right Hungarian party which formed a government in Hungary known as the Government of National Unity. They were in power from October 15, 1944, to March 28, 1945. The Final Solution to the "Jewish question" in Hungary got underway with a speed and efficiency surprising even to the Germans.

Between mid-April and late May, practically the entire Jewish population of the countryside was ghettoized. In the largest deportation operation in the history of the Holocaust, between May 15 and July 9, over 437,000 Hungarian people were transported to Auschwitz-Birkenau, where, upon arrival and after selection, they were killed in gas chambers by SS functionaries. Others were sent to work as slave labourers for German industries. The remaining 10,000–15,000 evaded capture by hiding, many in the forests, living as Gentiles, or taken in by others. The speed with which the Hungarian authorities cast out Jews from society, then robbed, segregated, and deported them, was unprecedented in the entire history of the Holocaust.

By early July 1944, the only Jewish community left in Hungary was in Budapest, mostly in the ghetto in Pest. A Jew living in the Hungarian countryside in March 1944 had a less than ten percent chance of surviving the following twelve months. In Budapest at that time, a Jew's chance of survival of the same twelve months was about fifty percent.

It was for this reason that my brother Avraham left the countryside to reside in Budapest. Avraham had moved to Hungary from Bratislava in 1929 and was a Hungarian citizen.

Germany's gradually deteriorating military situation, the wave of international protests, and the spreading of the news of the mass exterminations induced Horthy to stop the deportations in early July. Romania, which had been an ally to Hitler until that point, changed sides and declared war on Germany, which shook the Nazis' position in the region. Exploiting the situation, Horthy dismissed the cabinet and appointed a new government led by General Geza Lakatos. The new administration's main task was to leave the German alliance. The action was poorly planned and badly executed. On October 15, the Germans took the initiative, made Horthy resign, and put Ferenc Szalasi and his Arrow Cross Party into power. The new "Leader of the Nation" recommenced the deportations, and during November and December 1944, some 50,000 Jews from Budapest were deported.

It is most likely that my brother and Aranka's sister, together with her husband and son, were deported at this time. Elizabeth and Egon perished in 1944 at Auschwitz, as did my brother Avraham. Aharon was deported to Auschwitz and survived.

Elizabeth (Birji) Birnbaum, my mother's sister. Elizabeth's husband, Aharon, had a general store where they lived, in Putnok, Hungary.

Egon Birnbaum, son of my maternal aunt Elizabeth and her husband, Aharon Birnbaum. Egon and Elizabeth died in Auschwitz in 1944. Aharon was deported to Auschwitz but survived.

Sara and Yosef-Shalom (Joseph) Goldberger, my father's brother, on their wedding day. Joseph was on a transport that left Sered on March 29, 1942, to Majdanek, where he perished.

Moshe Tov-Yehia (age two) and Renate (age four) were with their mother, Sara Goldberger, on a transport that left Zelina on June 19, 1942, to Auschwitz, where they perished.

In 2007, my family visited Auschwitz. Here I am with my daughter Shira. Shira provided the photograph that adorns the cover of this book.

THE JEWS remaining in Budapest were locked up in two ghettos. Terror became constant in the capital, and Arrow Cross militiamen murdered thousands of Jews.

Before Easter, in the spring of 1944, my wife, son, and I were walking down a very nice street with a few friends from Czechoslovakia when suddenly, I saw the German army marching towards us. First, there were motorcycles, then cars, then heavy machinery and tanks. Already by that afternoon we heard that the city was filled with thousands of German soldiers. They, together with the Hungarian militia, gendarmes loyal to the Arrow Cross Party that had already been active for a long time, began immediately to round up the Jewish population. These Arrow Cross gendarmes would constantly beat up Jews, and we had to be very careful not to cross their paths. There were certain areas and streets of the city where the majority of the Jewish population lived.

During the occupation, the Germans ordered the establishment of a Jewish council in Budapest and severely restricted Jewish life. Apartments occupied by Jews were confiscated. Hundreds of Jews who lived in these areas were rounded up and interned in the Kistarcsa transit camp (originally established by the Hungarian authorities), fifteen miles northeast of Budapest.

I had to register with the authorities again on the last day of March 1944. It was just a week before Easter. I had a dilemma. If I didn't go, the police would most likely come for me and I would be placing my wife and baby in jeopardy. If I went, I really didn't know what would happen to me. Registering would only put me in jeopardy.

I spoke with my brother about the situation. He told me that he wanted my wife and baby to move to another place right away in case anything should happen to me. He also told me that he had the resources and would help Aranka and the baby obtain new identity papers that would show them as being Christian, not Jewish, in order to save their lives.

Trusting that Aranka and our son would be safe, I had no choice but to register. I went to the office and saw that there were many hundreds of people like me there. Everyone was interned and nobody was let out. They had prepared everything in order to deport us to Auschwitz. We were all taken to Csepel Island, twenty-five miles from Budapest, where we were interned until there were 3,000 Jews together to fill the transport.

Csepel Island was a huge industrial complex, called the Manfred Weiss Steel and Metal Works, which consisted of more than thirty-two factories. Founded by Baron Manfred Weiss of Csepel, a Jewish industrialist, by the time of World War I, the company was one of the largest defense contractors in Austria-Hungary, producing all types of equipment, from airplanes to automotive engines and cars. In 1911, it expanded its factories, and soon became the principal source of ammunition for the armies of Serbia, Bulgaria, Portugal, Spain, Mexico, and the Russian Empire.

By the outbreak of World War II, the company had become a modern industrial conglomerate, with over 40,000 employees. Its management remained largely composed of Hungarian Jews. When Nazi Germany overran Hungary in 1944, the majority of the management was arrested by the Gestapo. The Weiss family was allowed to immigrate to Portugal and escape the horrors of the Holocaust, but their large art collection, along with the entire industrial complex bearing their name, was taken over by Germany.

So it was here, in one of the factories, that we were interned. I had nothing with me. My brother heard about the internment and was able to smuggle a small bag to me by paying a bribe to someone. The bag contained food, some clothes, and a small pouch of money. I was wearing two gold rings and had a Schaffhausen watch on my wrist.

My brother told me that he was successful in moving my wife and son to another place as discussed, and that he had given them the money that I had prepared for her. I prayed that the same thing that happened to me would not happen to them.

Later that year my brother was deported to Auschwitz and perished.

Fifteen days later, we were all taken twenty-five miles away to the Keleti train station. We were met by the Hungarian gendarmes and taken to the loading area. Three thousand people were herded into railway cattle cars for transport to Auschwitz. There were one hundred people to a car, sharing a single bucket for waste and a single pail of water to drink. We travelled for a total of two nights and three days and arrived in Auschwitz on the evening of April 17, 1944.

There were suddenly barking dogs and lights shining in my eyes. I was still holding onto my bag and hadn't let it touch the filthy floor of the cattle car. I was able to walk out of the car but most of the others had to be hauled out.

We were divided into two lines: men in one, and women, children, and older men in the other. The man to my left was a Hungarian with a grey beard. He could hardly stand up and was pulling me to the left. He wanted me to go over to that line with him because he could see that these prisoners were going by truck to the camp. He could hardly stand up. Most of the people were sick and exhausted from the train. I tried to get him to come over to the men's-only line with me, but was unsuccessful.

We were moved forward in a line, four abreast. An SS officer, Dr. Josef Mengele, simply pointed his finger at each of us and said sternly, right, left, right, left. I was selected to go right. Another SS officer stopped me. He yelled at me in German to take off my rings and my watch, and to give him my gloves and anything else that I had in my pockets. I understood him, of course, because I spoke German perfectly. In the pouch I had 20,000 pengos and 300 US dollars. He took all my money too. We were marched to the camp, guarded by SS soldiers.

All our clothing, documents, and jewellery were taken. We stood there naked while they searched the crevices of our bodies and shaved our heads.

Then we went into the shower room. The kapo and his helpers collected our shoes while we had cold showers. I got a pair of wooden clogs, one that fit my foot and one that didn't.

Then, cold and wet and naked except for our clogs, we walked to the barracks—our new home, filled with bunk beds. One of the inmates recognized me. He was a friend of mine from Bratislava. He was so surprised to see me. He told me that of all our friends from Bratislava, he was the only one still alive. He told me about the crematoriums, that all the people who had come off the train and were directed to the left were by now gassed, and their bodies were going up in smoke. He told me that he saw my brother Joseph and his entire family perish that way. I felt sickened and could smell the burning flesh from within the barracks. He had survived because he had been involved with the Red Cross and wore the badge on his sleeve. He was so sorry to see me, especially now, because he was aware that the war was turning and he was certain that it would be over soon.

I told him what had transpired over the course of the past two years since I last saw him, and he told me the same. He told me that he wanted to help me and brought me a bowl with a little soup in it. I looked at the soup and I couldn't eat it. It looked and smelled awful. I was hungry but could not touch it and gave it to someone else. At that moment, I couldn't have predicted that in the future I would give anything for this soup.

He told me that if I wanted to stay alive, I needed to show that I was capable of working. The Allies were bombing German infrastructure and they needed men to repair the buildings, roads, and railways that were being hit. He told me that the next day there would be an appell, a twice-daily roll call, where they would have another selection from all the barracks looking for men who they could use for forced labour throughout Germany. This would be my chance to show that I was physically fit for work. If chosen, I would be given some food, a little bread and margarine every day, and would have a chance of surviving to the end of the war.

The prisoner's rations varied between concentration camps slightly, but by and large were the same in most labour camps. Inmates were fed three times a day. The goal of these rations was not to sustain the inmates, but to exploit them for labour with the minimal provisions possible. These were:

- **Breakfast:** half a litre of "coffee" (imitation coffee or ersatz coffee), which was boiled water with a grain-based coffee substitute, or "tea"—an herbal brew, unsweetened.

- **Lunch:** about a litre of soup, the main ingredients of which were potatoes, rutabaga (turnip), and small amounts of groats, rye flour, and Avo food extract. Most newly arrived prisoners were often unable to eat it, or could do so only in disgust.

- **Dinner:** 300 grams of black bread, served with about twenty-five grams of sausage, or margarine, a tablespoon of marmalade, or cheese. This bread was meant to cover the needs of the following morning as well.

This food ration was extremely minimal, containing almost no protein, hardly any vitamins or fats, and often caused diarrhea. This entire food ration contained roughly 800 to 1,500 calories per day. A prisoner in a heavy-labour detachment had a deficit of approximately 1,100 to 1,200 calories per day. This rate of depletion meant a weight loss of 4.4 to 8.8 pounds per week. The chief problem was that these meagre rations, over time, destroyed the health of the inmates. They then became more susceptible to diseases and infections. It remained the common goal of all inmates to avoid starvation. Hunger and fear were two of Hitler's most powerful weapons: to grow hungry slowly—not just to miss breakfast or to have a day of fast, but to really be hungry, to have less and less, day by day, month by month, so that at the end you only think about one thing, how to get something more to eat.

The next morning, we lined up again. We gave our names, birthdays, and other essential information, and they recorded our height, weight, and hair colour. I couldn't believe it when they tattooed our arms for identification purposes. We dressed in striped uniforms that, like the clogs, didn't quite fit, and we had no underwear, no socks.

Two prisoners arrived, carrying a large canister of hot tea, my first food or drink in days. It was awful but I drank my portion. After that, the prison workers inscribed our tattooed numbers on our clothing.

Next, we had the appell, the roll call. We were all lined up, hundreds of us. When my name was called I stepped forward. I was deemed capable of work, and sent to the right side. Those who looked frail or sick went to the left. These people were not seen again. That evening I made a promise to myself and to God that if I survived the war and was able to, I would arrange to be buried in Jerusalem when the time came.

The next morning we were woken and given a piece of bread and a little margarine. We were led to the railroad station and once again herded into cattle cars. We were taken to a place called Wustegiersdorf, which was a labour camp within the Gross-Rosen concentration camp system.

Gross-Rosen was originally a small concentration camp, which had been in existence from May 1941. A considerable enlargement of the camp took place in 1944. Apart from the main camp in Gross-Rosen, numerous auxiliary camps were created (approximately one hundred). They were mostly located on the territory of Lower Silesia.

The hierarchic structure of the concentration camps followed the model of Dachau, the first concentration camp, established in 1933. The German staff was headed by the Lagerkommandant (camp commander) and a team of subordinates, composed mostly of junior officers. One of them commanded the prisoners' camp, usually after being specially trained for this duty. Male and female guards and wardens of various kinds were subordinate to the command staff.

The prisoners had a hierarchy of their own. Prisoner-supervisors (kapos) were considered an elite that could wield power. The prisoners had different opinions about them. Most Jewish supervisors tried to treat their brethren well; some were harsh towards the other inmates.

The appell, the lineup that took place every morning after wakeup and each evening after returning from labour, was one of the horrific aspects of the prisoners' lives in the camps. We were forced to stand completely still, often for hours at a time, exposed to the elements in the cold, rain, or snow, and to the terror of sudden violence by SS men, guards, or kapos. The camp routine was composed of a long list of orders and instructions, usually given to all but sometimes aimed at individual prisoners. The majority of these orders were familiar, yet some came unexpectedly. All of one's strength had to be enlisted to overcome the daily routine: an early wakeup, arranging the bed's straw, the lineup, marching to labour, forced labour, the waiting period for the meagre daily "meals," the return to camp, and another lineup, before returning to the barracks.

There was a sort of black market in the camp. I exchanged a slice of bread for a bowl of soup. With that bowl of soup I went elsewhere and said, "Come on, give me two slices of bread for this." And somehow or other we organized ourselves this way.

The cooks would dole out the soup from barrels, and as you got to the bottom of the barrel, the soup got thicker. People would play strategic games to position themselves in the line in order to get the soup at the bottom of the barrel. You then came back and analyzed your soup. Was it thick or was it thin? How many pieces of meat did you find? A piece of meat could be traded for a piece of bread.

We were crazy for food; it was constantly on our minds. I would pretend that the food was like manna and when I would eat, I would imagine that I was eating my favourite foods from home. Even so, it was only the will to live that kept you alive; everything was really that fragile.

Prisoners in concentration and labour camps exhibited heroism and resourcefulness in their daily lives, struggling not only to maintain the ember of physical life, but also their identity, culture, humanity and basic moral values, friendship, and concern for others. These were what sustained their survival.

AS BELLA Gutterman explains in her book *A Narrow Bridge to Life*, "On June 10, 1943, the Allies mounted a heavy offensive against industrial plants across Germany. To mitigate the bombardment damage, the German authorities took far-reaching measures to decentralize the armaments plants, removing many factories from the central area to safer regions on the fringes of the Reich."

In 1944, following several military setbacks, the proliferation of labour camps intensified. The SS converted its other camp-based enterprises to war production. All the main camps, including Auschwitz, became hubs for the distribution of slave workers. The SS constructed new labour camps next to factories all over the Reich in order to accommodate the inmates allocated to them.

Many of these large German companies showed interest in using slave labour as early as 1941. In fact, 200 German companies had taken over half a million inmates from over a dozen different concentration camps. Some of Germany's most prestigious firms were on the list, including the automobile manufacturers BMW, Volkswagen, Auto Union, and Daimler-Benz. Others on the list included Siemens, AEG, Telefunken, IG Farben, and Krupp Industries.

Riese (German for "giant") became the code name for the construction project of Nazi Germany in 1943–1945. The hilly Sudetenland, sloping into Lower Silesia, was chosen as one of the appropriate safe locations for the construction of subterranean armaments plants. Many factories were relocated here.

The town of Gluszyca (German: Wustegiersdorf) and its vicinity was the location of many labour camps connected to Project Riese. From October 1943 to March 1945, manufacturing plants of Friedrich Krupp AG were relocated here from Essen. They took over two textile factories belonging to Meyer-Kauffmann Textilwerke AG, and adapted them to armaments production.

In most of the new camps, SS personnel supervised the inmates both in their living quarters and in their workplace. Preservation of an experienced, trained workforce became a priority in some of the new camps. Especially for Jews, allocation to a war production–related camp significantly improved their chance of survival.

In 1944, dissatisfied with the progress of the massive project, Adolf Hitler decided to hand over the supervision of construction to the Organisation Todt and assign the Jewish prisoners of concentration camps to work. Twelve labour camps for Jews were established. Some were in the vicinity of the tunnels constructed as part of Project Riese. The network of these camps was named Arbeitslager (AL) Riese, and was part of the Gross-Rosen concentration camp.

Gutterman writes, "Although each camp was different in nature, ... these were the harshest camps in the Gross-Rosen constellation. They were noted for high mortality and some of the poorest living and dietary conditions among all forced-labor camps in the National Socialist State."

The camp administration, including the commander of AL Riese, had its office in the camp known as Wustegiersdorf. About 13,000 prisoners worked for this project. They were all Jews and came from many European countries, but seventy percent were Hungarian. Most of them were transferred from the Auschwitz concentration camp. Nazi authorities wanted inmates capable of hard physical work. They most wanted young, strong, and healthy men. The first prisoners of AL Riese were registered in Gross-Rosen's file on April 26, 1944. Prisoners were assigned to different work, according to requests from the companies. The duties were mainly outdoors. Labour included cutting trees, and building roads, bridges, sewage systems, and most of all, boring tunnels. It was the hardest and the most dangerous work, and caused many fatal accidents.

MY WOODEN clogs caused injuries. My feet were always sore. We were plagued by fleas in the barracks. One of the hardest problems was the terrible winter cold. We pounced on paper bags that once held cement, and wore them as extra insulation under our jackets or shirts. Simply cut holes for your head and arms, and the damp and cold would not affect you as much.

The only way to survive with our meagre rations was to secure an extra source of food. On the way to work, when we passed fields, I would snatch a potato, a carrot, or a beet. I would hide them in sleeves or in special pockets that I sewed in my coat. I would always share this bounty with friends later on in the barracks. It was worth the risk.

Gutterman tells us that "hundreds of executions took place in the main Gross-Rosen camp." Public executions, by hanging or gunfire, were carried out from 1944 onward, mostly for attempted escape from labour camps.

We had many debates and discussions in our barracks in the evening. Members of the Zionist youth movement were interned and led discussions on Palestine. We did not work on Sunday, and there were prisoners who performed plays. Observant Jewish prisoners improvised Jewish calendars and we would hold services as best we could on the festival days and on Shabbat.

Every morning, we were marched on foot to our workplace by two SS commandos. Usually the work site would be a mile away. They monitored us while they carried rifles. Our only rest came at noon when we were given a little bread and tea. We received a small tin can and bowl to use for our meagre rations. By evening, after a day's hard labour, I had a little bit of soup and a little bread with margarine to look forward to.

Mortality was very high because of disease, malnutrition, exhaustion, dangerous underground work, and the treatment of prisoners by German guards. Many exhausted prisoners were sent back to the Auschwitz concentration camp. Documents list the deportation of 857 prisoners, as well as fourteen executions after failed escape attempts. An estimated total of 5,000 victims lost their lives. At the end of 1944, a typhus epidemic broke out among the prisoners.

Typhus killed millions of prisoners in Nazi concentration camps during World War II. The deteriorating quality of hygiene in camps created conditions where diseases such as typhus flourished.

WHILE I was working, I could hear the bombs and shelling get louder and louder. I was aware that the Allies were now fighting the Germans on German soil. Because the front line of the war was approaching, evacuation of the camps began in February 1945. The Nazis didn't want to leave evidence of crimes against humanity. These evacuations were also called death marches, as so many of the prisoners died slow, terrible deaths on these long walks. They died from starvation, exposure from wearing only pajamas in freezing temperatures, fatigue, and being beaten or shot to death.

We worked merely 8.5 miles from the city of Breslau. The fighting was intense when the Battle of Breslau began on February 13, 1945. We could see the airplanes above and the ground shook from the constant bombing and artillery.

The project we were forced to work on failed. In the face of an upcoming front, building of "Riese" was coming to an end. Those 4,000 or so prisoners who were still fit enough to walk from various camps, including Wustegiersdorf, were evacuated to Bergen-Belsen in February 1945. Another 4,775 men died during the evacuation. Some prisoners were left behind, mostly badly ill, until the Russian army arrived in the area in May 1945.

I HAD spent a total of ten months at this concentration camp. I had survived 303 days from the date of my arrival on April 20, 1944, to the date of my evacuation on February 16, 1945. I had endured so much pain and suffering. Hot and then freezing cold weather. There were two things which kept me going: my belief in God, my religion, and my prayers; and my wife and son.

I knew many of the daily prayers by heart. Throughout my youth and adulthood I put on tefillin and a tallit, and prayed every morning. I attended Shabbat services at the synagogue every week. I led the daily prayers in the morning and evening.

During my entire horrific ordeal, I would cover my head and say the following in Hebrew to myself three times prior to closing my eyes every night:

"Rigzu v'al techtau, imbru b'lvavchem v'al mishkavchem v'domu sela" (Take account of yourself, and do not sin; talk to your heart as you lie down to sleep, and may all be still).

And "Sh'ma Yisrael Adonai Eloheinu Adonai Ehad" (Hear, O Israel: the Lord is our God, the Lord is One).

In the morning when woken I would recite the following to myself each and every day:

"Mode ani lifanekha melekh chai v'kayam shehechechezarta binishmahti b'chemlah, rabah emunatekha"

(I give thanks before you, King living and eternal, for You have returned within me my soul with compassion; abundant is Your faithfulness!) and followed with the Sh'ma once again.

At noon, when I was given a brief respite from work, I would often think of the following words in the Tahanun prayer in which David said to Gad (one of the personal prophets of King David):

"I am greatly distressed; let us fall into the hand of God, for His compassion is great, but let me not fall into the hand of man. O, You who are compassionate and gracious, I have sinned before You: O God, full of compassion, have compassion upon me and accept my supplications."

During the day, I thought many times of the promise that I had made to God that I would be buried in Jerusalem. Not somewhere without a proper funeral. Not up in smoke like my father and brother. I would think of the Amidah, the silent prayer at the centre of Jewish daily prayers, which the Talmud instructs us to use to express our needs to God. I would pay special attention to the verse that reads: "Have mercy, Lord, and return to Jerusalem, Your city. May Your Presence dwell there as You have promised. Build it now, in our days and for all time. Re-establish there the majesty of David, Your servant. Praised are You, Lord who builds Jerusalem."

Whenever I felt as if I could not go on any longer, I would say to myself the words, "chazak v'ematz"— "Be strong and of courage." Be strong and of good courage; be not afraid, neither be thou dismayed: for the Lord thy God is with thee wherever you go.

The second thing that kept me going was my desire to see my wife and child again. I thought about them every day, all day. The most horrible thing was not knowing how they were, what had happened to them since the day I last saw them. Andrew would be two years old in a few months. What did he look like?

4

AURELIA

(1944-1945)

AVRAHAM WAS crying when he told me that David was being deported, after he was made to register. I was so worried about the future. Andrew was ten months old. Avraham gave me new identification papers for Andrew and myself. Our last names were no longer Goldberger. Andrew now had a girl's name. Avraham gave me a necklace—a cross to wear around my neck at all times. I had taken on the identity of a widowed Christian woman with a baby girl.

We were taken to a Christian home where Avraham had arranged for us to live. We were given a nice room in the house and were greeted and treated very warmly by the owner. Avraham knew this person and he felt that we could live there in safety. He paid her a lot of money that David had given him to pay for our room and board. She had prepared girl's baby clothing for Andrew to wear. Andrew's hair was long and beautiful. It was imperative that Andrew be dressed as a girl in case we were ever stopped by the gendarme. They would check any suspicious boys for circumcisions.

That year, I worked at the hospital where Andrew was born. The doctor who delivered Andrew took pity on us and was able to get me the job. I trusted him. I had nursing experience and was able to help him out. For this work, I was given some money to buy food, but more importantly, had access to medicine and milk for my baby. The doctor was fine with me bringing the baby to the hospital. Whenever I couldn't bring him along, I left Andrew with the lady at home. She treated him as if he was her own.

Avraham did not come to see us, as he did not want to give us away to the authorities, should they be following him. I was able to see my sister once in a while. She helped me out with money, to help me pay the owner of the house. Later in 1944, I no longer saw or heard from her, or her son Egon.

In October 1944, the Arrow Cross takeover of Budapest took place. In fewer than three months, death squads killed as many as 38,000 Hungarian Jews. Arrow Cross officers helped Adolf Eichmann re-activate the deportation proceedings from which the Jews of Budapest had thus far been spared, sending some 80,000 Jews out of the city on slave labour details and many more straight to death camps. Virtually all Jewish males of conscription age were already serving in the Hungarian army's forced labour battalions.

I was witness to many of these atrocities, and scared for our lives. What if they found out we were hiding as non-Jews? I witnessed as Jews were loaded on to freight and cattle cars at the station. I heard their cries, but could not help. I witnessed as Jews were beaten up and murdered in the streets, but could not help. Every time I heard a knock at our door, I was afraid this would be the end.

I kept busy knitting clothing for Andrew and mending and cooking for the lady in the house. One day, I was walking to work with Andrew in the stroller, taking our regular route. As we turned the corner a block away from the bridge, a friend called out from her kitchen window. She motioned with her hand that we should stop by for a short visit. She came out and we chatted for a while. Suddenly we heard a loud noise and the ground shook. The bridge on which I would have been walking with Andrew was bombed and blown to pieces. Our lives were spared because this woman had called me.

This bombing was to go on for many months and I really don't know how we survived it all. Hungarian and German soldiers were running everywhere in the city. The noise never stopped. I was so afraid of Andrew getting hurt all the time and I didn't know if we would ever see David or any of our family ever again.

THE SIEGE of Budapest was one of the bloodiest operations of World War II. The Russian army started its offensive against the city on October 29, 1944. More than 1 million men, split into two operating maneuver groups, advanced. On December 26, 1944, a road linking Budapest to Vienna was seized by Russian troops, thereby completing the encirclement.

As a result, nearly 33,000 German and 37,000 Hungarian soldiers, as well as 800,000 civilians, became trapped within the city. Refusing to authorize a withdrawal, Adolf Hitler had declared Budapest a fortress city, which was to be defended to the last man.

Until January 9, 1945, German troops were able to use some of the main avenues as well as the park next to Buda Castle as landing zones for planes and gliders, although they were under constant artillery fire from the Russians. Before the Danube froze, some supplies could be sent on barges, under the cover of darkness and fog.

Nevertheless, food shortages were more and more common, and soldiers had to find their own sources of sustenance, some even resorting to eating their horses. The extreme temperatures also affected German and Hungarian troops.

In mid-January, Csepel Island was taken, along with its military factories, which were still producing Panzerfausts and shells, even under Soviet fire.

On January 17, 1945, Hitler agreed to withdraw the remaining troops from Pest to try and defend Buda. All five bridges spanning the Danube were clogged by traffic, evacuating troops, and civilians. German troops destroyed the bridges on January 18, 1945, despite protests from Hungarian officers. One of them was the famous Chain Bridge, dating from 1849.

Budapest's defenders asked permission to leave the city and escape encirclement, but Hitler refused. German troops could no longer hold their ground and they were forced to withdraw on January 28, 1945, abandoning much of the occupied territory.

Unlike Pest, which is built on flat terrain, Buda is built on hills. This allowed the defenders to site artillery and fortifications above the attackers, greatly slowing the Soviet advance.

On February 11, 1945, Gellert Hill finally fell after six weeks of fighting when the Soviets launched a heavy attack from three directions simultaneously. Soviet artillery was able to dominate the entire city and to shell the remaining Axis defenders, who were concentrated in less than one square mile and suffering from malnutrition and disease.

On the night of February 11, 1945, some 28,000 German and Hungarian troops began to stream northwest away from Castle Hill. They moved in three waves. Thousands of civilians went with each wave. Entire families, pushing prams, trudged through the snow and ice.

The remaining defenders finally surrendered on February 13, 1945. Budapest lay in ruins, with more than eighty percent of its buildings destroyed or damaged, historical buildings like the Hungarian Parliament Building and the Buda Castle among them. All seven bridges spanning the Danube were destroyed. Overall, more than 500,000 Hungarians were transported to the Soviet Union (including between 100,000 and 170,000 Hungarian ethnic Germans).

Some 38,000 civilians died during the battle, which lasted from December 24, 1944, to February 13, 1945 (one month, two weeks, and six days). About 13,000 died from military action and 25,000 died from other causes such as starvation and disease. Looting and mass rape were carried out by Russian and Hungarian criminals.

ANDREW AND I had endured constant artillery bombardment and street-by-street tank and infantry battles. We spent our nights in bomb shelters. Our daily rations consisted of melted snow, horse meat, and 150 grams of bread. The home in which we had been sheltered was damaged. It was time to give up our false identities, find another place to live, and find out what was happening with David.

The streets were full of people trying to figure out what to do. I found the building where my uncle Jakob (Birnbaum, my father's brother) had an apartment. It had been damaged, but luckily, it was still standing. I went to the basement suite of the caretaker and he was still there. He recognized me and was able to give me a place to stay. Andrew was able to dress as a boy again. He was walking and talking at the age of twenty-one months. I had been bartering my clothes for milk to sustain Andrew through these horrific times. I found the location of the Jewish Centre, where a Hungarian Jewish relief organization was set up to assist Jewish survivors in the city. I reported to the centre and registered our names on the list of survivors.

The National Committee for Attending Deportees, or DEGOB, was founded in March 1945 in Budapest.

Its activities covered three main areas: repatriation of thousands of Hungarian Jews who had been deported, aid activities including providing food and clothing, and documentation activities for registering the names of both the survivors and the dead.

I wanted so much to know what had happened to David. It was now close to the beginning of March 1945, and I last saw David on March 31, 1944. I decided that I would go to the Jewish Centre every day to try and learn his whereabouts. I had his picture in my purse.

5

DAVID

(1945)

As THE Allies approached, our camp was evacuated. I was sent to Bergen-Belsen on February 17, 1945. Bergen-Belsen was a Nazi concentration camp in what is today Lower Saxony in northern Germany, southwest of the town of Bergen near Celle. Originally it was established as a prisoner-of-war camp, and in 1943 parts of it became a concentration camp.

In December 1944, SS-Hauptsturmfuhrer Josef Kramer, previously at Auschwitz-Birkenau, became the new camp commandant. In January 1945, the SS took over the POW hospital and increased the size of Bergen-Belsen. As eastern concentration camps were evacuated before the advance of the Russian army, at least 85,000 people were transported in cattle cars or marched to Bergen-Belsen. Before that, the number of prisoners had been much smaller. In July 1944, there were 7,300; by December 1944, the number had increased to 15,000; and by February 1945, when I first arrived, it had risen to 22,000.

Bella Gutterman gives a detailed account of this evacuation:

The column that reached Bergen-Belsen was so large that it was now separated into two subcolumns. The smaller one comprised 800 prisoners from Wolfsberg and a contingent from Wustegiersdorf. On the morning of the first day (17 February 1945), the prisoners set out in ranks of five, towing equipment wagons. Their route was identical to that of the column that preceded them, and they spent the night at and near the Friedland camp. The next day (18 February), they continued to follow the route of the previous column and reached Chelmsko. There they were housed in two silos crammed so full that the gates of one of them collapsed under pressure, burying fifty-six people alive. On the third day (19 February), the column headed for the border of the Protectorate. Its destination was the Trautenau railroad station via Parschnitz.

On the road from Choustnikov Hradiste to Parschnitz, in the vicinity of Konigsdorf (Dvur Kralove), twelve common graves were found after the war. When [the graves] were examined in August 1945, the investigators found shreds of clothing and serial numbers of Jews who had been interned at Wolfsberg and Schotterwek. Some of the bodies showed no signs of injury; these people had died of exhaustion. Other bodies, however, had shattered skulls, and many had gunshot wounds. Since these corpses had been buried in two graves at two different points in time, the investigators adduced that at least two evacuation columns had passed the location. The graves contained 179 corpses, whose serial numbers indicated that two-thirds were Jews from Poland and the others were Jews from Hungary.

After a 21-kilometer [13-mile] march and a brief rest in Chelmsko, the prisoners reached the train station in a state of severe exhaustion. According to one prisoner's testimony, the evacuees were placed aboard a train on 19 February and were still in the cars on 25 February. The exact date of their arrival in Bergen-Belsen is not known.

WE WERE not given any food or water for the trip. We were 100 to 120 people crammed into each car, and we were forced to stand. It was freezing on the train. Every freight car had at least ten to fifteen people who died.

We pulled into the Dresden train station. There were ditches alongside the tracks and the dead bodies were dumped overboard into the ditches straight from the rail cars. They even removed the lousy pajamas from the dead before dumping the bodies. Dresden is very close to the Czechoslovakian border. When we passed through one Czech town, some people tried to offer us loaves of bread by throwing them into the rail cars. They knew that evacuations were taking place. The SS wouldn't allow them to do this. They threatened these nice people by telling them that they would be shot if they continued. And we hadn't had anything to eat in days. In some other towns we passed through, open cars laden with frozen prisoners, people were not upset with what they saw. They stood and stared apathetically. It did not occur to them to offer food and assistance.

When the train arrived in Bergen-Belsen, I was placed in the barracks with most of the able-bodied men who had survived the terrible conditions. We were given a very meagre ration upon our arrival. In the distance we could hear bombing in and around the city of Hannover, 28.5 miles away.

We spent two nights in Bergen-Belsen before being loaded onto flatbed trucks. Each crowded truck had two SS officers inside. The train station at Hannover had been almost completely destroyed by heavy bombing the day before. Many other buildings and homes in the area were destroyed as well.

We were taken to Hildesheim, fifty-two miles away. In March 1945, there was a satellite of the Neuengamme concentration camp system in Hildesheim. The Neuengamme system had more than eighty-five satellite camps, which were established all over northern Germany for construction projects and armaments production. The prisoners had to do hard labour for the war economy. Living and working conditions were murderous. All together, at least 42,900 people died in the Neuengamme main camp and satellite camps, or died on death marches when the camps were evacuated.

The Hildesheim camp held around 500 Jewish prisoners. These prisoners carried out railway work for the Hannover regional railway office, and rebuilt the city's freight yard, which had been severely damaged by Allied bombs. Most of the prisoners were from Hungary. The men were housed in the local civic hall. The commanders of the satellite camp were SS officers who were responsible for the camp's administration, while the prisoners were guarded during work by members of the Volkssturm (Nazi militia).

We were stationed at the railway building, and had the task of rebuilding the railway. The work was very difficult, but at least we were given some food to sustain us. Every night we slept at the civic theatre hall. One morning as we left the hall, there were many who were too sick to work and had to be left behind. When we returned later that day, we saw that the entire building had been destroyed by bombs. I saw arms and legs and all kinds of body parts all over the place, amongst the rubble. I was so lucky to have been able to work that day.

Now there was no place to sleep, so they took us to the Leine River, where we tried to sleep on the roadside beside the water. We were freezing in only our striped pajamas.

On March 22, 1945, another building housing prisoners was destroyed by Allied bombs, and the freight yard was severely damaged again as well. The SS, under threat, planned to evacuate the work camp and leave for the Hannover-Ahlem satellite camp, then from there to Bergen-Belsen. The Hannover-Ahlem work camp[2] was also part of the Neuengamme system, and was a forced labour camp for a large industrial company.

I was one of the 340 prisoners who arrived in Hannover-Ahlem from the Hildesheim work camp on March 25, 1945. We joined the 750 men who were still alive there. Evacuation of Hannover-Ahlem began on April 6, 1945, with 600 prisoners being marched to Bergen-Belsen. Those 250 prisoners who were not well enough to march were left behind. We reached Bergen-Belsen on April 8, 1945; several prisoners were shot on the way.

We marched during the day as the SS officers kept an eye on us. In the evenings, we stayed overnight in the barns of farms. One of these barns had food stored away, and the starving prisoners ate some of the corn and whatever else they could find amongst the hay. In the morning, the farmer told the SS officers that food was stolen. Right away an appell was called, and the SS shot every tenth name that was called. During this roll call dozens of prisoners were shot on the spot.

When I was taken to Hannover, the number of prisoners at Bergen-Belsen was 22,000—in a camp originally designed to hold about 10,000 inmates. In the short time that I was away, the population had increased to 60,000. There wasn't even a single blade of grass to be seen. The overcrowding led to a vast increase in deaths from disease, particularly typhus, as well as tuberculosis, typhoid fever, dysentery, and malnutrition. All inmates were subject to starvation and disease.

THERE WAS an incident in Bergen-Belsen in 1944 that involved Dr. Israel Kasztner. Kasztner was a Hungarian Zionist leader in his native Transylvania and then in Budapest after Transylvania was annexed by Hungary in 1940. In late 1941, he helped found the Relief and Rescue Committee of Budapest. Until the spring of 1944, the committee successfully smuggled refugees from Poland and Slovakia. It was a person from this committee who helped Aranka and me with the plan to come from Bratislava to Budapest.

Kasztner contacted the SS officers in charge of the Final Solution in Hungary. Soon thereafter, he made his offer to exchange "blood for goods," whereby a certain number of Jews would be spared in exchange for large amounts of goods. Kasztner negotiated directly with Eichmann and later with Kurt Becher, another Nazi official.

Kasztner had convinced Eichmann to release some 1,700 Jews. Kasztner and other Jewish leaders drew up a list of Jews to be released, including leading wealthy Jews, Zionists, rabbis, Jews from different religious communities, and Kasztner's own family and friends. They were transported out of Hungary on June 30, 1944, on what came to be known as the "Kasztner train." After being detained in Bergen-Belsen, passengers on the "Kasztner train" eventually reached safety in Switzerland in December 1944.

One morning, a few days after I entered Bergen-Belsen, some trucks carrying Hungarian Jews arrived at the camp. These folks may have had an indirect relationship with Kasztner, but they weren't on his original 1944 transport. They were all dressed in regular clothes and looked to be much better off than the rest of us. I really didn't know what they were doing in Bergen-Belsen. Perhaps they spent a great deal of money to bribe the Germans? There was an old man on one of the trucks who saw me. He was elderly and could hardly walk. He called out to me in Hungarian to come closer. He told me that they were being taken to a train station for transport to Switzerland. He told me that if I wanted to save myself that I should join him on the truck and make like I'm his son. He wanted to save my life.

I figured this to be a wonderful thing, and as the trucks got ready to depart I jumped in next to him. At that moment, an SS officer approached and looked at me. It was very easy to see that I was out of place, as I was wearing striped pajamas, and everyone else wore regular clothing. In German he said, "What are you doing here?" I told him that the man next to me was my father. He took his rifle and hit me hard with the butt right in the side of my face. I thought that I would die from the pain.

He pulled me down from the truck and threw me onto the ground. There was nothing I could do. He dragged me over to a guard in a watchtower beside the barbed-wire fence. He punished me by making me stand there, in a crouched position with both of my hands on my hips. He told me that the guard in the tower would be watching me, and that if I moved away, he had orders to shoot me on the spot. I stood in that position for the entire day without any water. The sun was shining and it was terribly hot.

The sun went down and I was still standing. I was in such pain that I decided I had had enough and needed to get back to the barracks. I thought to myself, *What do I have to lose? If I go and he shoots me, so be it.* Standing there all day I saw lots of planes flying overhead, and several times wished that they would drop a bomb and end this nightmare for me. This was the first time that I completely lost my will to live. How much suffering can a man endure? I was always very strong in my beliefs and optimistic about life. I needed to find out what happened to my wife and son. So I stood up and made my way back to my barracks. I was not shot.

There was nothing to eat and no water to drink. I just lay there in the barracks, starved, tired, sore, and lifeless. I felt as if I were half dead. My weight was about sixty-five pounds and I was skeletal. I'd had nothing to eat or drink for a long time and I couldn't even stand up anymore.

WHEN THE British and Canadians advanced on Bergen-Belsen in 1945, the German army negotiated a truce and exclusion zone around the camp to prevent the spread of typhus. On April 11, 1945,

Heinrich Himmler (the Reichsfuhrer-SS) agreed to hand the camp over without a fight. SS guards ordered prisoners to bury some of the dead. At around one o'clock in the morning on April 13, an agreement was signed, designating an arc of nineteen square miles around the camp as a neutral zone. Most of the SS were allowed to leave. Only a small number of SS men and women, including camp commandant Kramer, remained to "uphold order inside the camp." The outside was guarded by Hungarian and regular German troops. Due to heavy fighting nearby, British troops were unable to reach Bergen-Belsen on April 14, as originally planned. The camp was liberated on the afternoon of April 15, 1945.

When British and Canadian troops finally entered, they found over 13,000 unburied bodies and around 60,000 inmates, mostly acutely sick and starving (including in the satellite camps). The prisoners had been without food and water for days before the Allied soldiers arrived, partially due to Allied bombing. Immediately before and after liberation, prisoners were dying at a rate of around 500 per day, mostly from typhus. The scenes that greeted British troops were described by the BBC radio:

> Here over an acre of ground lay dead and dying people. You could not see which was which ... The living lay with their heads against the corpses and around them moved the awful, ghostly procession of emaciated, aimless people, with nothing

to do and with no hope of life, unable to move out of your way, unable to look at the terrible sights around them... Babies had been born here, tiny wizened things that could not live... A mother, driven mad, screamed at a British sentry to give her milk for her child, and thrust the tiny mite into his arms, then ran off, crying terribly. He opened the bundle and found the baby had been dead for days.

The reporter stated that this day at Bergen-Belsen was the most terrible of his life.

Initially lacking sufficient manpower, the British allowed the Hungarians to remain in charge and only commandant Kramer was arrested. Subsequently, SS and Hungarian guards shot and killed some of the starving prisoners who were trying to get their hands on food supplies from the store houses. The British started to provide emergency medical care, clothing, and food.

Immediately following the liberation, revenge killings took place. While I was lying down, I witnessed the killing of the kapo who was in charge of our barracks. He was a terrible Hungarian who would yell and hit the helpless. He would eat food in front of us while we were starving. He took joy in making others do demeaning things. Without any SS to help him out, he was defenseless as the enraged inmates swarmed upon him, knocked him to the floor, and kicked him until he was motionless.

The British forced the former SS camp personnel to help bury the thousands of dead bodies in mass graves. Some civil servants from the nearby town of Celle were brought to Bergen-Belsen and confronted with the crimes committed on their doorstep. There were massive efforts to help survivors with food and medical treatment. Despite their efforts, about another 9,000 died in April, and by the end of June 1945, another 4,000 had died.

I WAS part of a group of nineteen interned young men and boys, all from Czechoslovakia. I had a friend, Oren Lutska, who I went to school with in Bratislava. He had gone to London to train with the British Legion. He was one of the liberators, and he recognized me. He said to me, "David," and I was too weak to even talk. He picked me up with his hands like a rag doll and took me to his room. There he had milk and cookies that he gave me. I stayed with him in his room for a few days. He gave me the most nourishing food to help get me on my feet again.

My friend offered me three packages of cigarettes. I didn't smoke, but I knew that these would be good to barter for other things such as food. I was lucky that I had never smoked. It wasn't until after the war that I started.

When the liberators came, they gave everybody two cans. One of the cans contained what looked to be pig fat. The other can was pretty good; it had candy, chocolate, and cookies. People were so hungry that they ate the fat. I had spoken with two brothers from Hungary the day before, and they were in all right health. When I saw them that day, they were both dead. They ate the fat and their stomachs could not handle it. I tried my best to warn people not to do this.

The British troops and medical staff tried these diets to feed the prisoners, in this order:

- **Bully beef from army rations.** Most of the prisoners' digestive systems were in too weak a state from long-term starvation to handle such food.

- **Skimmed milk.** The result was a bit better, but still far from acceptable.

- **Bengali Famine Mixture.** A rice-and-sugar-based mixture which had achieved good results after the Bengal famine of 1943, but it proved less suitable to Europeans than to Bengalis because of the differences in the food to which they were accustomed. Adding the common ingredient paprika to the mixture made it more palatable to these people, and they started to recover. Some were too weak to even consume the Bengali Famine Mixture.

I was already feeling much better, and I could see what was going on in the camp. I saw that typhus was running rampant and that people were dying like flies.[3]

The Russian and Ukrainian people would go out of the camp to the countryside and get chicken and pork and bring food back into the camp for themselves.

They could do this because the guards at the camp were Russians and Ukrainians. They were not letting anyone else out at the time for fear of spreading typhus.

I gathered the eighteen boys and men from Czechoslovakia together and said, "They are telling us that we are now free, so if we are free we need to get out of here now. If we stay here, there is so much disease all around us that we may never leave alive." I told them that I had been in Hannover and knew that it was very close to us, and that between us and Hannover there was nothing but farms. If we could get to Hannover, we could start to figure out how to get back home. I was able to convince everyone in the group that this is what we should do. Some were very weak, but I told them that we have to be strong and that this is something that we could do if we all did it together.

I went to one of the commanding British officers and told him (speaking in German) that I had a group of nineteen from Czechoslovakia, and that we wanted to go home. I told him that I was a married man and that we all had families that we wanted to find. I told him that we needed to leave because of the typhus in the camp and that people were dying.

He replied that this was not possible, that we would have to wait until the Slovakian legion came for us. I told him that if that was what we would have to do, then we would not make it out alive. Yugoslavia was the only government that came and rescued its people. They had come with trucks and took all of their citizens. I knew that Slovakia had nothing, certainly no trucks, and that if we had to wait for them we would contract typhus and die. Slovakia had paid the Germans to get rid of us. However, the officer would not relent.

I gathered the boys and told them what the officer said. We had to have a plan in place to get out. It was already the beginning of May, and there was a beautiful full moon out. The camp was in the shape of a large circle. Barbed-wire fencing surrounded the entire camp. It was a Saturday evening. I told them that we would go for a walk around the perimeter of the camp, and if we saw the opportunity, we would sneak out. Everyone agreed.

Nobody slept that night. We got up at three o'clock in the morning and walked around the entire camp. Ukrainian guards were stationed all around the fence and we got scared. We went back to the barracks and spent the whole day talking and sleeping. I told everyone that we needed to try it again that night.

As we walked around that next night, I noticed that a hole was cut at the bottom of one of the fences; a person would be able to slide right under. I realized that this must have been the way that the Russian and Ukrainian people were able to leave and return to the camp. I took out one package of menthol cigarettes and gave it to the Ukrainian guardsman. At the same time, I took one of the boys and pushed him through the fence to the other side. The guard didn't say a word. So I took the second person and the third and the fourth until we all got out. It was early Monday morning around four o'clock. I separated the boys into two groups of nine.

I had walked almost the whole way from Hannover to Bergen-Belsen once before. For sure all of the farms along the way would have milk, bread, and butter. I told one group to go up the left side of the road and the other group to go up the right side. I told them that one person from the group should go and knock on the door of the farmhouse and ask what they can give us for breakfast. I said, "Ask nicely and don't ask for too much. If anyone refuses, then give them hell and let them know who we are, where we came from, and make a demand." Most people were very nice and some were arrogant. The arrogant ones would get scared of us and then give us something as well.

On the roadside I saw a pile of personal belongings. Amongst the items were two prayer books. I rescued them from the rubble.

I had a very good friend in the group, Fritzi Green. He was older than me, a former druggist, and a wonderful guy. One day he pulled a gold tooth out of his mouth in exchange for a little bit of soup and he shared it with me. Shortly after we left the camp, he became very ill, dropped to the ground and could not walk. He had come down with typhus. It turned out he had eaten a little piece of pig and contracted the disease. He lay down on the ground and didn't have the strength to move. I thought, *My goodness, now we are free, already a few miles away from the camp, and this had to happen.* He began to cry and said that we should leave him behind and make our way to Hannover without him. He said that there was no way that he could be helped and that I should take the other boys right away and save ourselves. I told him that I would never leave him alone.

It was early morning, and I saw a farmer in his horse and buggy travelling down the road on the way to work. I spread the boys out across the road so that the farmer would have to stop. I told him that we have a sick man that needs to be taken to the hospital right away. He said that he needed to get to work and could not help.

With that I started to yell at him. I told him that all of this was because of Hitler and explained what had been done to us. I told him that if he didn't take the man to the hospital, together with whoever else could fit on top, then we would take his horse and buggy and do it ourselves.

We put Fritzi on top of the wagon and went directly to the hospital in Hannover. How lucky and happy we were to discover that the doctor working at the hospital was from Prague; his name was Professor Koch. Fritzi would go on to stay in this hospital for two months. Dr. Koch looked after him and gave him the finest medicines. Antibiotics were relatively new, and Fritzi received them. He regained his health, and when I saw him in Bratislava a couple of months later, he told me that he was able to return there on his own.

On the wagon with us was a young sixteen-year-old red-headed boy named Aaron Feld. While Fritzi was in the hospital, I took Aaron under my wing. In Hannover, soup kitchens had opened all over the city. We could get a room almost anywhere that we wanted. People knew what had happened to us, the concentration camps, the starvation, and the slave labour. They knew that we were desperate.

We were able to knock on the door of a home and ask people for a room—many times we would "demand" a room. Usually the request was granted together with an apology for all the suffering that we had gone through. They wanted to help and would even cook for us.

I watched over Aaron as if he were my son as he was only sixteen. There was a bank located on the main floor of a building in the city. On top were residences where Aaron and I shared a room. Others from the group who left Bergen-Belsen together did the same in different areas of the city. One day, we made a plan to meet for lunch in our room at noon. I came back at noon and got worried, as Aaron didn't show up. I waited until three o'clock, when he suddenly arrived. I was relieved to see him and asked what had happened. He told me that he had been walking down a street and saw a sign on a building reading "Dr. Echstein." He hadn't wanted to tell me, but that morning, his stomach was bothering him. He went into the doctor's office and told the nurse that he wasn't well and would like to see the doctor. The waiting room had twelve to fifteen patients waiting.

The nurse told him to sit down and went into the doctor's office to tell him that there was a young boy who came in who looked like he might have been in a concentration camp. The doctor looked out the door and asked him to come in. Ten minutes later he called for the nurse to tell all the others in the waiting area that they would have to go home as he needed to attend to this patient and it would take the rest of the afternoon. The doctor was an older man of about seventy years of age. Dr. Echstein was with Aaron for hours. He wanted to know about everything the boy had experienced.

When Aaron told him about me and the way I took him out of the camp and to Hannover, he said that he wanted to talk to me the next day. He gave him some drugs to help his stomach. I was very relieved to hear that Aaron was all right. He told me that the doctor really wanted to see me and that we should go to his office at one o'clock in the afternoon the next day. So we did. Again, his waiting room was full of people, and again, when the doctor saw us, he told his nurse to send everyone home because he needed to spend time with us.

He locked the door, as he didn't want to be disturbed. We sat and talked for a while. He then looked at me and said,

Mr. Goldberger, I have two sons. I'm an old doctor, and I wanted to try and organize the people against what was going on. I wanted to demonstrate at city hall with others who opposed the Nazis. But

I couldn't trust anybody. I was afraid for my life. I was scared of my own sons. I had to close the door and curtains when I turned on the radio to hear the news from London. I knew what was going on. Mr. Goldberger, I want you to know that I am ashamed of being a German. I was afraid that my own sons would kill me. They were both SS officers. I want you to know that I will be writing a book about this, because I am now a free man and can talk about the terrible things that happened.

At this point he started crying. He wanted to help us with anything. He offered me money, he offered me clothing, he offered me anything I wanted. "What can I do for you? How can I help?"

He helped me by talking to us about the way he felt. He helped by being so kind to us. He helped by being truly remorseful for what the Germans did as a nation to the Jewish people. I did not accept any of his material offers. He pushed one hundred Reichsmarks into each of our hands. I really didn't want money, but he insisted. Money at that time wasn't worth anything. If I saw this note lying on the street, I wouldn't even have picked it up.

After World War II, the Reichsmark continued to circulate in Germany, but with new banknotes (Allied Occupation Marks) printed in the United States and in the Soviet Occupation Zone. There were also new coins without swastikas. In practice, massive inflation dating back to the latter stages of the war had rendered the Reichsmark nearly worthless. It was supplanted by a barter economy, commonly known as "cigarette currency."

As we walked out of his office and down the street, I noticed a name on a large building. We used to do business with this company. We had purchased a great deal of woolen fabric from them for our store in Bratislava. I walked in the door and introduced myself. I looked around and saw that the place was mostly empty. There was damage to the building, and broken windows had been taped up. At the end of the war, ninety percent of the city centre was destroyed, with fifty-two percent of buildings heavily damaged or completely destroyed.

Two owners came to the front and asked how they might be able to help me. I told them what had happened to me over the course of the past two years. I said that we had just come from Bergen-Belsen, and that I wanted to go home to Bratislava and find out what happened to my wife, my child, my father, and my brothers. They told me that they knew what had been done to the Jewish people and asked if they might give us some money to help. Again, I didn't want any money.

I said to them, "If you really do want to help me, then I would appreciate it if you could give me a couple pieces of cloth." I had nothing. Money was worthless. With some cloth, I would be able to go to a farm and barter for some milk, bread, butter, and eggs for my wife and child if they were still alive. They told me that they had two pieces of cloth put away, two times three metres of suiting wool, and they graciously gave that to me.

With these two pieces of cloth from Hannover I returned to Budapest and was able to start my life once again.

THE FIRST thing that I wanted to do was find out if my wife and child were still alive. From Hannover, there was no way to communicate with the outside world. We needed to go elsewhere to be able to get information. So all of us, except for Fritzi, went to the railroad station in order to make a trip to Prague. The railway was not running, but there were loads of supply trucks making their way to Prague, driven by American soldiers. We were lucky to be able to hitch a ride with these trucks. Prague was 300 miles away.

Aaron and I got a room in a Prague hostel that was set up for returning refugees. They gave us some food and a little money. They also provided us with a document that would enable us to travel, and a free ticket to Bratislava from Prague. I told Aaron that I didn't want to go back to Bratislava or Budapest until I knew what happened to my wife and child. I asked him to go without me, find out, and send me a telegram with the news. If they were alive, I would go; if not, I would never go back to either place again.

A day later I got a telegram from him saying that my wife and son were alive in Budapest.

I couldn't wait to leave and meet up with him in Bratislava. I was able to get a train that evening and arrived in Bratislava early in the morning. Aaron was waiting for me there. He told me that he had seen a mutual friend of ours, Cohen Lozi, who had been travelling every day from Budapest to Bratislava and back again. He had seen my wife in Budapest pushing a stroller with my son. I immediately bought a ticket and waited all day for the train that would take me to Budapest.

I arrived in Budapest very early the next morning and went to the Jewish Centre, where people had been registering their whereabouts. The office was still closed, so I rested on a park bench nearby. I was tired from all the travelling and I didn't know where Aranka was staying. I had a newspaper covering my eyes as I rested. The sun hit my eyes, and as I took the newspaper off, I saw a lady walking towards the building with a little boy in a stroller. It was Aranka and Andrew. That's how we were reunited. Thank God, we had all survived.

We went back to the room where Aranka and Andrew were staying. This had been our uncle Jakob's apartment. The caretaker knew my wife, as we had visited here in the past. Also, the caretaker was worried that he might get in trouble should any of the owners come back and find that he hadn't given Aranka a room.

My uncle Jakob had been deported and did not survive. He had two sons who did survive and returned to the building in Budapest: Aharon Birnbaum, who lost his wife, Aranka's sister, would go on to Israel. He remarried there and had a daughter whose name is Esti (named after Elizabeth). The other son, Albert (Shani) Birnbaum, would immigrate to America in 1956 and settle in Los Angeles.

I had arrived in Budapest with only the two pieces of fabric I received in Hannover and a few Czech korunas to my name. That is all. My wife was so skinny, so very thin. She told me that she had been going to the Jewish Centre each morning and showing my picture to returning survivors from the camps. Aranka would ask everyone if they had seen me. Many people told her that they had seen me and that I was either killed or had died from starvation. But she never gave up hope.

Foreign aid was now flowing into Budapest for the thousands of surviving Eastern European Jews who were coming to the city every day. This aid provided food, clothing, and money for shelter. Most of the aid was coming from the American Joint Distribution Committee/Joint Jewish Agency for Palestine, the National Jewish Relief Commission, and DEGOB, which were all integrated into the National Jewish Aid Committee, or OZSSB.

6

DAVID
with
AURELIA
(1945–1948)

W E WERE now free to move around the country, and I needed to start to make a living for my family. Vienna was not far from Budapest (150 miles), and had a severe food shortage. The countryside with its farms had food to eat, but the cities, especially Vienna, had almost no food at all.

My cousin and I came up with the idea of exchanging the two pieces of wool for food in Budapest and trading for other goods in Vienna. We picked up different kinds of salami and other food items and made our way by open truck to Vienna with the hopes of trading the food for saccharin, jewellery, and cigarettes. With these items you could buy anything you wanted. Money was worthless at this time. You would need a barrel full of paper money to buy a piece of bread. At the height of the inflation, prices were rising at the rate of 150,000 percent per day. The government had stopped collecting taxes altogether because even a single day's delay in collecting taxes wiped out the value of the money the government collected.[4]

We had packed the food into two small suitcases. When we arrived in Vienna, we went door-to-door with the food. I was very naive in setting the value of certain merchandise. One woman traded a gold ring for some food. I later found out that the ring was not gold.

We went to Saint Michael's Church to ask for a place to sleep because we couldn't afford a hotel. We gave the church minister a little something and he let us sleep there.

The next day we peddled some more as we needed to keep going until the food was gone. At one house, I picked up a beautiful small pocket watch with a chain. Right away I thought to myself that this was something that I wanted to keep as a Bar Mitzvah present for my little boy. I decided not to barter it. I kept it for that purpose.

We returned to Budapest with the merchandise we had bartered—saccharin, cigarettes, jewellery—and traded it back for more food items, like salami. Once again, we made the trip to Vienna, and once again we had success in trading for items that were useful to turn a profit in Budapest.

We travelled at night in an open truck. Russian soldiers were all over the roadside. They would sometimes have too much vodka to drink and would stop the trucks, steal people's goods, and beat them up, even killing some civilians. This happened to us. A group of soldiers stopped our truck and told us to get down. We refused, and they tried to pull us out of our seats. They beat me with their fists and hit me with their rifle butts and stole all of the items that we were taking back to Budapest. I used all of my strength to hold onto the wheel of the cart—it was a wonder that we survived the beating and that God gave me the strength to hold on. Even after the war we were still fighting for our lives.

We returned to Budapest with nothing to show for all of our hard work. My dream of starting up again was finished.

Aranka and I decided that it was time for us to return to Bratislava. With the crazy inflation in Budapest, it was impossible to do any business. The currency in Czechoslovakia was much more stable than in Hungary. Right after World War II, in 1945, the country returned to the Czechoslovak koruna. Previously, the country had been divided by the Germans, and we had the Slovak koruna. It was a safe environment to do business in.

Aranka's sister Magda was back in Bratislava, and she was alone. Being the older sister, Aranka wanted to look after her. Both Aharon and Shani were already making plans to leave Europe for Israel and the United States. There was no reason for us to remain in Hungary any longer.

On June 15, 1945, I received some money from DEGOB that would enable the three of us to travel back to Bratislava and rent an apartment somewhere in the city.

The Jewish community of Bratislava had by now renewed its activities. There was a steady stream of

My beloved aunt Magda, in approximately 1939.

Jewish Slovak refugees returning from the camps; the community opened temporary hostels for them and set up soup kitchens.

We reunited with Magda, and the four of us rented a very small apartment at Hurbanovo 17. We didn't have any furnishings at all, so we had to sleep on the floor. It was a tiny old place without a working elevator and we had to walk up ten floors. Within the next few weeks, with the help of the Jewish relief agencies, we were able to get beds for the apartment, and over time, we furnished the apartment with what we needed. We were also able to get the toys and clothing that we needed for Andrew as he grew. Andrew went daily to a kindergarten class where he was able to make new friends. We all watched him perform at a Hanukkah concert with his classmates.

Both Aranka and Magda were having a very difficult time dealing with the tremendous losses in their family. Thank God they had each other. Magda loved Andrew so much, and together they played beautifully. Andrew brought some joy into our lives again.

I made contact with my brother Mayer who was in Cuba, and told him of our family's losses during the war. Without asking for anything, Mayer sent me some money to help start my life again. He was so happy to hear that I was still alive and together with Aranka and Andrew. He wrote that he now had four lovely children in Cuba by the names of Rosa, Luba, Albert, and Fanny. Also that our brother Morris had two daughters, Elvira and Flora.

We were very close to my mother's sister Magda (top left), who lived with us in Bratislava after the war. Magda loved Andrew so much, and together they played beautifully.

My uncle Morris's two daughters, Elvira and Flora, in Cuba, date unknown.

AGAIN, I needed to start making a living. Slowly, I started with a friend who gave me some goods on consignment that I could trade and turn a profit with. I did this for a short time.

I met with another friend who had been in the same business as me before the war. His last name was Brown. We decided that we would set up a wholesale-only textile business in the warehouse district of the city. We called our new company "Succos," which translates to Feast of Booths, a major Jewish festival that commemorates the shelter of the Israelites during their forty years in the wilderness.

I had wonderful connections to fabric suppliers and mills before the war. I made a trip to Moravia and Bohemia to re-establish these connections. I also filled out all the necessary forms to import fabrics for our company. I next went to see if any of our wholesale customers from before the war had survived and were interested in re-establishing their textile businesses. I found that approximately ten percent of the business owners had survived and were in dire need of merchandise to start their lives again. They were unable to secure any merchandise because of shortages. At the end of the war the European economy had all but collapsed, and much of the European industrial infrastructure had been destroyed.

These small business owners trusted me completely and gave me money up front in order to supply them with merchandise. With this money, I travelled to Bohemia and Moravia once again. With my connections still in place, I bought quantities of fabrics and had them shipped to the warehouse we had set up in Bratislava. Brown was in charge of the warehouse while I did the travelling. In time, we had set up a very lucrative wholesale textile business.

Both Brown and I knew that life in Czechoslovakia was going to be a temporary situation for the two of us. Firstly, there was still tremendous antisemitism throughout the entire country. I saw this with my own eyes as I travelled to different areas. The people were both surprised and upset to see Jewish survivors. They were worried that the stolen Jewish homes and household items that they had been given by the previous government would be taken back. We had to be very careful once again, in our own country. Slovakia was still a very dangerous place for a Jew. We had to be cautious when walking alone on the streets, especially at night, because there were frequent attacks against Jews. Our plan was to make enough money to afford the luxury of immigrating to North America.

Aranka and I began to prepare the necessary documentation. All of our documents had been taken away from us. On January 14, 1946, I was able to obtain personal identification papers for myself. In August of 1946, we were able to obtain duplicates of Aranka's, Magda's, and Andrew's birth certificates and our marriage certificate. In 1947, we obtained passports.

Magda wanted to go back to Spisske Vlachy and find out what had happened to her family home. In the spring of 1946, we took the train together. The general store that Josef had for over thirty years had been taken over by a tailor. The house was now occupied by a Roma family. The situation in the town was terrible. Everyone saw us as foreigners. Nobody remained from Magda's childhood. We explained the history of the store to the tailor, who was very afraid of us, and we demanded just three months' rent, which he paid. He was very relieved to see us leave.

We were in touch with relatives in New York, Vancouver, and Cuba. Aranka's Uncle Harry and Auntie Etta wanted us to come to Canada. They said it was a lovely place to live. They were well-connected and offered to sponsor us. Uncle Harry's family was in the furniture business, and they would do everything possible to help us settle in the community. It sounded lovely and was far away from the horrors of Europe. That's where we decided to go. They started the paperwork for all of us.

Everything was ready, and we were planning to leave in early 1947. Aranka was pregnant again, and we were expecting a baby sometime in March. It was now October 1946. Aranka's uncles Harry and Mano (in Toronto) told us that it would be too dangerous to make such a lengthy trip while she was in her last trimester, and said that we should wait until sometime after the birth. So we put our plans on hold.

In March of 1947, Aranka gave birth to our second boy. We named him Joseph Shalom after Aranka's father Josef and my brother Yosef-Shalom. The Goldsteins were Joseph's godparents. Birji Goldstein had taken Magda under her wing in the sewing area of Auschwitz to help her survive the war.

We were now a family of four. We had moved into a larger apartment sometime before Joseph's birth in anticipation of our larger family. Bratislava, Palisady 48, would be our final residence in Czechoslovakia.

WE HAD built up a nice wholesale business, and by doing so had helped hundreds of survivors get back on their feet. I continued to travel, and Brown continued to run the warehouse. There were new laws put in place by the government with new quotas on imported fabric. On one of my buying trips in late 1947 to Moravia, I was able to purchase a very large amount of fabrics. Once again, I had pre-sold the entire amount.

The goods arrived at our warehouse in three large trucks on a Friday at noon. Brown and I, together with our hired help, worked on the orders the entire weekend. On Monday morning, the delivery trucks arrived at the warehouse to pick up the goods. Our entire warehouse was empty. Everything had been shipped out.

Across the street there was a small café. People in the area looking for wholesale merchandise would go there during the day for coffee, breakfast, and lunch. That Monday, a man having lunch at the café received a tip from his waitress: she had seen huge trucks delivering goods to our warehouse on Friday, and thought he should check it out. She knew we were Jewish.

My father, David Goldberger, in 1946 after liberation. This photo was taken for his identification card in Bratislava.

Aranka's Uncle Harry and Auntie Etta wanted us to come to Canada, where they had moved before the war. They said it was a lovely place to live. They were well-connected and offered to sponsor us when we moved to Vancouver in 1948.

Uncle Harry was born in Hanusovce nad Top'lou and Auntie Etta was born in Svidnik, Czechoslovakia.

Me with my mother, Aurelia, called Aranka, in 1947.
We were in Bratislava at this time.

Me in Bratislava in 1947.

Andrew and me in 1947. This photo was taken in Bratislava, soon before we moved to Canada.

The man came over and said that he would like to see the merchandise that had recently come in. We had nothing to sell and told him that we were unable to help him. He then reported what happened to a government official, whose ministry sent two detectives to investigate. They came into our office and said that they would like to have a look around our warehouse. We let them in and they were astounded to see that it was empty. They wanted to know where the large shipment was. I told them that the fabrics were all paid orders and showed him all the invoices together with the names of our customers and addresses of the shipments. They looked through the invoices and asked why all of the customers were Jewish. They wanted to know why nothing was being shipped to non-Jews. During the war, all of the Jewish business had been taken over by Gentiles, and they did not see a single one of these "new owners" on our list of customers. They said that it was against the law to only do business with Jews and took us to the office of the local jail.

It was mid-December, just before Hanukkah. We were kept in jail for two days before we were able to go home. We had proved to the authorities that we had the official stamp on the order for export from Moravia. Furthermore, we proved that the entire shipment had been pre-sold. Even though we had proved our innocence, the local newspaper did a story on the front page outlining what had happened. The newspaper twisted the story and accused us as only selling to the new Jewish storekeepers.

It was definitely time for us to close the business and leave the country once and for all. I wanted to leave as soon as possible and never return to this land of terror and blood.

Brown had made arrangements to be with family in New York. Before he left, I gave him money in US dollars to hold for me. I told him that when I got to Vancouver I would contact him with an address to wire the funds. I would need this money to make a fresh start once again.

Aranka's Uncle Isak (Isi) and Aunt Sara were living in Antwerp, Belgium. He told us that we should leave as quickly as possible and that we could stay with them until we were able to secure passage on a boat to Canada. Uncle Isi had survived the war in England.

Aranka, Magda, Andrew, Joseph, and I left for Antwerp in mid-February 1948, approximately ten days before the communist takeover of Czechoslovakia. Andrew was four years, nine months old and Joseph was eleven months old.

We were in Antwerp for a total of three months. Charles and Anna Gold (Riff) and their two children, Claude and Mimi, were also in Antwerp. Uncle Isi and his family were so kind to us. Uncle Isi fell in love with Joseph. He loved to pinch his cheeks. Antwerp had been heavily bombed during the war, and there was still rubble everywhere. Andrew and Claude loved to play in the rubble and dug tunnels in the earth together with Mimi. Every night before bedtime, they would have a contest to see who could drink a glass of milk the quickest.

Andy and me in 1948 in Antwerp, before going to Canada.

Anna Gold (née Riff), Aurelia's auntie, survived the Holocaust with her husband, Charles, and their two children, Claude and Mimi. They went to North America at the same time we did, in 1948, though they settled in Seattle.

R.M.S. "ASCANIA."

We left Liverpool on June 5, 1948, on the RMS *Ascania* and arrived in Canada eight days later. We stayed a few days in Montreal and then took the train to Vancouver.

My parents and brother in Montreal in 1948, having arrived
by ship from Liverpool.

Aurelia's uncle Mano was waiting for us in Montreal and saw us off as we boarded the train to Vancouver. None of us could speak a single word of English. Here he is with his nephews in 1958.

WE HAD left Czechoslovakia just in time. The country was forced to become a Soviet satellite state in February 1948, via a communist coup.

MOST OF the ships going to North America were already full, as soldiers from the United States and Canada were returning home by the thousands. Therefore, it took quite some time before we were able to get passage.

We left Antwerp in May 1948. Charles and Anna and their two children left at the same time. They were going to settle in Seattle. We travelled from Antwerp to Liverpool and then from Liverpool to Montreal. We left Liverpool on June 5, 1948, on the RMS *Ascania* and arrived in Canada eight days later. We stayed a few days in Montreal and then took the train to Vancouver. Uncle Mano was waiting for us in Montreal and saw us off as we boarded the train to Vancouver. None of us could speak a single word of English.

We arrived in Vancouver on a beautiful, sunny, warm day. Even though we were all very exhausted from the long journey, we felt as though a jolt of energy had been shot inside our bodies. We were so very excited to finally be here and to start our new lives in Canada.

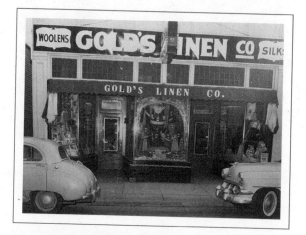

Gold's Linen Co. store on Granville Street in Vancouver in the 1950s. It was later changed to Gold's Fashion Fabrics.

Right to left: my dad, David Goldberger; Andrew (Bundi) Raab; and the first salespeople David hired at his original fabric store in Vancouver, Mrs. Hoffman and Mrs. Moseley, 1950.

Gold's Fashion Fabrics in 1971, located at the corner of Granville Street and 11th Avenue.

Our family in the backyard of our house on W. 42nd Ave in Vancouver. Left to right: (front) Joe, Judith, Andrew; (back) Aurelia and David.

IN 1952, Andrew came to me with a book that he'd seen Joe looking through. Joe was five years old. This was a very special book from Europe that I hid inside a bolt of cloth on a shelf high up in my office.

This book reminded me of how much I owed to this country and to the community of Vancouver. My dreams have all come true. It has been a long journey from the darkness of Europe to the brightness of Canada. I know that if I had remained in Czechoslovakia, my life would have been short-lived.

The people of Vancouver gave me a chance for a new life. Time has gone by so quickly, and as I make this statement in 1984, at the age of seventy, I thank God for all that he has helped me with. God bless the nation of Canada.

POSTSCRIPT

DAVID

MAY THEIR *memory be for a blessing.*
All told, over sixty members of our family perished during the Holocaust.

For most survivors, after dealing with basic needs like food, clothing, and shelter, their most important objective was searching for relatives.

We learned that in Aranka's immediate family:

Her sister Dorothy (Dodke) and husband Carl Roth from Czechoslovakia perished in Auschwitz.

Her sister Gisella (Gisi) from Czechoslovakia perished in Auschwitz.

Her sister Elizabeth (Birji) and nephew Egon from Hungary perished in Auschwitz.

Her father Josef and stepmother/aunt Eva from Czechoslovakia perished in Auschwitz.

Her sister Magda had miraculously survived three years in Auschwitz and was alive.

Aranka's uncles and aunties:

Sari Riff married Emmanuel Reichman in New York before the war.

David Riff perished in the Shoah.

Helene Riff perished in the Shoah.

Kina Riff perished in the Shoah.

Etta Riff married Harry Klein in Vancouver before the war.

Eva Riff perished in the Shoah.

Emmanuel (Mano) Riff survived and moved to Toronto.

Isak (Isi) Riff survived and was living in Antwerp.

Anna Riff survived with her husband Charles Gold and their two children, Claude and Mimi. They went to North America at the same time we did.

My immediate family:

My father Heinrich (Chaim) from Czechoslovakia perished in Sobibor.

My brother Yosef-Shalom, together with his wife Sara and their two children, Renate and Moshe Tov-Yehia, all perished in Auschwitz and Majdanek.

My brother Avraham (Pinchas) from Hungary perished in Auschwitz.

Mayer brought Morris, Sara, and Louisa to Cuba. Mendel went to Palestine. They were all able to be far away from Europe during the Holocaust and survived. Louisa moved to America and served as a riveter in an airplane factory during World War II. Both Mayer and Morris became doctors and were active in the

Jewish community in Havana. Sara eventually moved to America, as did Mendel.

Others:

Andrew (Bundi) Raab was together with me at the slave labour concentration camp at Wustegiersdorf, and we both survived.

Aaron Feld, the boy who I cared for from Bergen-Belsen, moved to Israel. I tried to find him later in Israel but was unsuccessful.

My mother's sister Dorothy, who married Carl Roth from Czechoslovakia. They both perished in Auschwitz.

Sara and Isak (Isi) Riff with their children in 1961. Isi was one of Aranka's uncles. We stayed at their home in Antwerp before coming to Canada.

Andrew (Bundi) Raab and David both survived the slave labour concentration camp at Wustegiersdorf.

Bundi was born in Komarno. Later he married my mother's sister Magda. Here they are with my parents. This photo was taken in Vancouver in 1987.

EPILOGUE

JOE

(2020)

DAVID AND Aurelia Gold would go on to build a new life in Vancouver. David built up a large family business and would become a legend in the textile industry in Canada. He was active in many Jewish organizations. Aurelia lived for her family, loved all of humanity, and enjoyed cooking and knitting.

Another dream was fulfilled when Aurelia gave birth to a beautiful girl, Judith Rose, who was named after David's and Aurelia's mothers. She is married and had a child and two grandchildren.

David and Uncle Harry sponsored Andrew (Bundi) Raab to immigrate to Vancouver. He and Magda were married, and later Magda gave birth to a beautiful daughter.

Harry and Etta, along with Bundi and Magda, would come to us for Shabbat dinners.

David, Aurelia, and their children travelled to Seattle for Claude's Bar Mitzvah.

David would visit with his brother Mayer in Florida, and later in Jerusalem.

Left to right: Joe, Aurelia, Judith, David, and Andrew
in Vancouver in 1950.

My father's sister Sara, with sons Samuel and Ignacio.

My uncle Mayer's daughters, Rosa, Luba, and Fanny, with
David's sister Sara, in Cuba.

A proud David and Aurelia with their three children, and David's
sisters Sara and Louisa, on the front steps of their home on
W. 42nd Ave in Vancouver. We moved to this house in 1953.
We played in the forest near us that is now Oakridge Centre, a
shopping mall.

Albert (Shani) Birnbaum helped my parents settle in Budapest by bringing them clothing and hosting them at his apartment while they found a place to live. He later settled in Los Angeles.

All of David's and Aurelia's immediate family members who
perished in the Holocaust were made honourary citizens of Israel.
Their memories are dedicated on a large rock that overlooks the
Yad Vashem Beit K'nesset sculpture garden in Jerusalem.

During the 1950s and 1960s David's sisters Sara and Louisa would visit and stay with us in Vancouver. On occasion, Sara's two sons, Ignacio and Samuel, would visit.

When making a trip to New York with Andrew and Joe in 1955, David was reunited with his brother Mendel, and met his nieces Rosa and Luba (Mayer's eldest daughters). On the way back through Toronto, he was reunited with Uncle Mano.

After retirement, David and Aurelia lived in Israel for two years. During this time (the mid-1970s) David was reunited with many survivors who were friends and business associates from Czechoslovakia. One day, while waiting at a traffic light in Jerusalem, a man came up from behind David, and without seeing his face, put his hands on his shoulders and said, "This must be David Goldberger. I would recognize these shoulders anywhere." It was his tailor from Czechoslovakia before the war.

David and Aurelia went to Uncle Isi's child's wedding in Jerusalem and reunited with many of Aranka's relatives.

It was at this time that David purchased a burial plot in Jerusalem, in order to fulfill the promise he'd made. His brother Mayer also had a plot in Jerusalem.

Shani Birnbaum came from Los Angeles to visit David, Aurelia, and their family in the summer of 1980.

Andy moved to Israel in 1962 to study at The Hebrew University. He made aliyah and lives with his wife. They have two children, and are blessed with five grandchildren.

All of David's and Aurelia's immediate family members who perished in the Holocaust were made honourary citizens of Israel. Their memories are dedicated on a large rock that overlooks the Yad Vashem Beit K'nesset sculpture garden in Jerusalem. May this be their final resting place and may they be in peace.

The Vancouver Holocaust Education Centre has in its possession the two prayer books that David recovered on the road from Bergen-Belsen to Hannover after liberation.

David and Aurelia's survival gave life to three children, seven grandchildren, and sixteen great-grandchildren.

JOE

(2020)

I am writing this book at the age of seventy-two, more or less the same age that my father was when he gave the oral testimony of his experiences during the Holocaust to Dr. Robert Krell in 1984.

I AM WRITING this book at the age of seventy-two, more or less the same age that my father was when he gave the oral testimony of his experiences during the Holocaust to Dr. Robert Krell in 1984.

The events of the Holocaust, and my family's experience, played a key role in my life. For as long as I can remember, I have thought of the Holocaust every day. Every morning when the water from the shower hits my head, I remember. Whenever I have any pain, be it physical or mental, I think of what my parents went through, and the pain seems to subside somewhat and the problem that is bothering me all of a sudden becomes trivial.

My parents did the best they could to put the trauma and loss of the Holocaust behind them. It was impossible. Throughout their lives, I witnessed and felt the moments when they were brought back to that place. I saw their faces change, and for a certain length of time they were different. They were no longer my parents as I knew them. Sometimes it would be a silent sadness, at others, a loud rage. Although I was not physically present during the Holocaust, I have been emotionally changed by it forever.

My father always felt cheated by the governments of Europe for the way he and his family were treated after the war. He settled for a very small amount of reparation shortly after coming to Vancouver. It wasn't so much the small amount as the fact that, when he later realized that he should have received much more, the German government consistently denied his attempts to right the situation. This became an ongoing issue in our family, and my brother and I would deal with it together for a half century.

As a result of our laborious efforts, further reparations were achieved, most disbursed between 2002 and 2006. My mother was not so concerned about this, but it was an ongoing subject for my father, and that kept our efforts alive. It was not so much the amount that mattered to him, but the recognition of wrongdoing. My parents were in an assisted living situation at the beautiful Weinberg Residence when most of our breakthroughs occurred. We were able to fulfill my father's wishes during his lifetime.

The reparations included payment by the Generali Insurance Company that my grandfather had placed on his life for my mother and her sister. My father had to surrender this insurance policy to the Germans at a bank in Bratislava.

Further reparations were finally made by the German government for the slave labour that my father suffered at the hands of the nation's industries.

Finally, the Slovakian government accepted a claim for seizure of property for the loss of my mother's family store and home in Spisske Vlachy.

All the proceeds from these reparations were donated to the Vancouver Holocaust Education Centre.

Again, it wasn't the amount that was important. What was important was the sense of closure that my parents were given.

WHEN I turned sixty in 2007, my wife Karyn and I took our family on a heritage tour to Eastern Europe. It was during our visit to a Jewish Museum in Budapest that I was drawn to a set of pictures that had been enlarged and placed on plexiglass to form dividers between the different rooms. I had seen some of these very same pictures somewhere before. When I asked the guide where they were from, she told me that they were taken from the *Auschwitz Album*. Yes, some of these were the same pictures that were in the book that I had seen in my father's office when I was five years old. I had not seen these pictures in fifty-five years. My heart was pounding.

She told us that the *Auschwitz Album* is the only surviving visual evidence of the process leading to the mass murder at Auschwitz-Birkenau. The photos were taken at the end of May or beginning of June 1944, either by Ernst Hoffman or Bernhard Walter, two SS men whose task was to take identification photos and fingerprints of the inmates (not the Jews who were sent directly to the gas chambers). The photos show the arrival of Hungarian Jews.

When my father was in the camps, he vowed to himself and to God that if he survived the war and was able to, he would arrange to be buried in Jerusalem when the time came. He made numerous trips to Israel after the war, and is pictured here at the Wailing Wall in 1975.

Grave of David Gold on Har HaMenuchot in the hills of
Jerusalem, Israel. (Last name was shortened from
Goldberger to Gold in Canada.)

Later we travelled to Krakow and went to Auschwitz. It was a cold and drizzly day, just as I had imagined it would be. We did a memorial service in the vicinity of the crematorium ruins. I noticed a very smooth, egg-shaped stone on the ground. For whatever reason, I bent down, took the stone, and placed it in my pocket.

Later that evening, when we returned to our hotel, we received a phone call from Vancouver telling us that my mother had fallen seriously ill. We cancelled the remainder of our trip and left the next morning for Vancouver.

My mother passed shortly thereafter. At the funeral, I took the stone out of my pocket and placed it in the grave. She was ninety-one years old.

MY FATHER always had a soft spot for the poor, for the orphaned, and for newcomers—most likely because he had experienced all of this himself during his lifetime. In 1955, he helped a great many Jewish refugees from Hungary. He gave some jobs, for others he found jobs. He helped them fill out papers and to find homes to live in. He treated these people as if they were his own family. He did the same for many families that emigrated from Chile.

My father was a philanthropic man. During his lifetime, he donated substantial sums of money to institutions in both Vancouver and throughout Israel. He appreciated the country of Canada and loved the state of Israel. In many instances, my brother and I had the honour of helping our father with these gifts through a foundation that he had set up. Other gifts my father made directly by himself. Most of this was done anonymously. However, my brother and I have learned over the years that his philanthropic gifts were significant.

My father taught me many important lessons in life. Charity was one of the lessons he taught by example.

My father passed in October 2010, and was buried in Jerusalem as per his promise to God in Auschwitz. He was nearly ninety-six years old.

My father had always talked about writing a book about his life. He was never able to do that. I hope that in some small way I have done him justice and provided closure for that unfinished business.

The Album

One aspect of writing this story was the possibility of coming across the book that I first looked at in 1952, at the age of five. Finding this book has been a journey unto itself.

In November 2019, while I was doing research for this book at the Center for Jewish History in New York City, I came across a book that was located in the Rare Books and Special Collections of the Vancouver Holocaust Education Centre. I froze, because the cover of the book showed a photo that looked like the book I had found in that bolt of fabric. It was frayed and tattered in the same way. I noted that the book was gifted by Mona Kaplan in 2011 as part of the Sam Kaplan collection.

Sam Kaplan was the owner and editor of the *Jew-ish Western Bulletin* in Vancouver and a very good friend of my father. I was elated, as I thought I had solved the mystery of what happened to the book! All I had to do was visit the centre in Vancouver on my return home, and after sixty-seven years, I would once again be holding the book in my hands.

It was the first week of January 2020 when I stood in a room at the Vancouver Holocaust Education Centre awaiting the staff who was retrieving the book from a locked cabinet. My heart was thumping. The book was placed on the table in front of me, but it was not the one. On the book's cover was a photograph of the book I remembered. This was an original first-edition printing of the *Auschwitz Album* from 1981. As I flipped through its pages, I noticed a few pictures that had been etched in my memory. The search for the book would continue.

I discovered that the person who found the orig-inal album in 1944, Lili Jacob, knew that she had something of value. Already, by word of mouth alone, its existence had become widely known. The Jewish Museum in Prague reopened on June 26, 1946. Lili sold some photographs to the museum that year. The museum made reproductions of the 203 photographs from the album. One copy of each was sent to the Jewish Museum in Budapest.

In 1946 and 1947, one of the main activities of survivors was searching for any evidence or documen-tation of lost loved ones.

At this time, my father was spending a great deal of time in Bohemia and Moravia on buying trips, and would most likely have heard of the album, as most of the photos showed Jewish people from Czechoslovakia. He certainly would have gone to the Prague museum, and there is a good chance that he may have purchased a book with many of those photos, as well as photos from other camps, such as Bergen-Belsen. He would have wanted to identify family or friends in those photos. Many photos taken after liberation by the British Army were available to museums by that time. A book showing photos of Auschwitz and Bergen-Belsen would have been of great interest to my father.

It is my belief that he did in fact obtain one of the early printed books in 1947 and brought it with him to Canada in 1948.

In order to find out if this was a possibility, I decided to contact the Jewish Museum in Prague.

I remembered that a former Talmud Torah classmate of mine, Leonard Barak, had moved to Prague many years ago. Although we had had no contact for at least sixty years, I was able to obtain his email address and reached out to him. His reply came back in fifteen minutes.

"Your email was quite a surprise, like a spirit from the past in more than one way. Your story is important and intriguing."

He sent me the email address of someone from the Prague museum and suggested that I contact him personally.

Martin Jelinek, from the Photo Archive department, wrote back to me:

"If you are thinking about an older book, there is a book of photos from the *Auschwitz Album* that were presented for the first time (1949) called *The Tragedy of Slovak Jewry*. Our museum did not publish any books about this album."

Martin also sent me a link to Winner's Auctions, where there was a copy of this book for sale.

I clicked the link. It had just been sold.

The book's description was: "pictures and documents, published by the Documentation Institute of the Union of Bratislavian Communities. Bratislava, 1949." It is replete with antisemitic posters and documents from the time of the Holocaust, and photos of atrocities done to the Jews (difficult to view), forced labour, SS units in action, destruction of synagogues, local Jews with yellow stars, death trains, selections, death pits, dead bodies hanging, photos of the liberating armies, and refugees.

So, if this was the book, then my father did not bring it from Europe, but would have obtained a copy of it when he was already in Vancouver.

How could I see a copy of this book?

I searched the internet and found the book through the WorldCat library system. It was available for in-person viewing only at six universities and institutions. These locations were in Los Angeles, Ann Arbor, Washington DC, Philadelphia, Amsterdam, and Marburg, Germany.

So, this was in fact a rare book, difficult to obtain. I figured, of all the places in the world where I might have a chance of purchasing a copy of this book, Jerusalem might be my best bet. In my search of bookstores in Israel, I found one, Bookstore Jerusalem Blum, which had a copy available for sale and listed as: "*The Tragedy of Slovak Jewry: Photographs and Documents*, Bratislava: Documentation Centre, 1949. 142 pp Hebrew and English; pages 17–42 are all black-and-white photographs, small tears on cover. Hardcover, 28 cm."

I immediately placed an order.

Twelve days later, a package arrived in the mail. The package was wrapped in brown paper, scotch-taped, and had twine wrapped around the parcel to hold it together. It reminded me of how my father prepared packages for mail in the store when I was a young boy.

I carefully opened the package, removed the bubble wrap, and held the book in my hands. The cover had the same frayed edges and the pages looked brownish with age.

I was once again a five-year-old boy in my father's store, looking through the pages of a horrifying book. But this was different; I was looking with the eyes and brain of a man in his seventies, who understood what his father and mother had been through, to bring that book to me.

It was as if my father was watching from above and had sent the book back to me from Jerusalem saying, "It's okay now, you are old enough to see this again."

The Letter

On July 6, 2020, I received an email from my publisher advising me that the final copyedit for this book had been completed. But the very next afternoon, something amazing happened.

I went into our storage room to look for a countertop to use as a temporary desk. As I pulled the countertop away from the back wall, it revealed a metal shelving unit where, twenty years ago, I had placed storage boxes. On one of the banker's boxes I had written, "Dad's office stuff."

I decided to have a quick look inside the box. Along with little "chachkas" and old magazines were some photographs, mostly duplicates of photos I had already put together for this book.

One was from a cruise to Israel that my parents had taken in the early 1960s, on a ship called the SS *Shalom*, on the ZIM Line. Cruise ships often take pictures of their guests meeting the ship's captain and place the photo in a nice folder or frame as a keepsake. I opened the folder and looked at the picture, it was a duplicate of one that I already had. However, when I pressed down on the photo, I felt something underneath it. Carefully, I removed the picture from its folder, and sure enough, there were papers folded underneath. Amongst the papers was a handwritten letter that I had never seen before.

The letter was written in English.

My dad loved to "dictate" letters. He would often say to me, "Joe, I want to dictate a letter to you. Be sure to make a copy for me to keep."

My parents loved going on cruises. Here they are on a cruise
to Israel in the 1960s.

This letter must have been dictated to an English speaker, as my dad did not yet speak English at the time of its writing. As I read it, I could tell that it was written after the war, in Bratislava, sometime during the fall of 1945, and mailed to Mayer in Cuba. The letter was to his brothers and sisters in Cuba. In it, my father writes about the period of the Holocaust, about the family lives that have been lost. That he is now married with a child, and of the hardships they endured and the very difficult times they are now in.

The letter reads:

My dear brothers and sisters,

We received your telegram and were glad to hear that you are all well.

We are quite well, thank God! I shall now describe our experiences to you in brief.

In the year 1939, Mayer sent me an immigration permit, then advised me to marry.

In the year 1941, I married, followed you, but it was not possible to immigrate. In 1942 the hard times for us began; then began the deportations of the Jews to Poland. In 1942 we lived with my wife's parents during the Easter holidays, then we came back to Pressburg [Bratislava], and transports were already being sent off, in which Schalom [Yosef-Shalom (Joseph)] lost his wife and two children. Seeing that our lives were in danger, we immigrated to Hungary. We had a bad time of it there; we were interned. Pinchas [Avraham] was in Munkacs, I brought him to Budapest. But he was constantly on duty as a soldier. He helped us very much, he procured us documents through which we obtained a leave of absence from the internment camp. In the meantime, my wife had a son. At the time, I was in a working camp; those were hard times for us. In 1944, the Germans came to Hungary, then they took me prisoner, and sent me to Auschwitz. It was good luck for me that they took me alone, for my wife and child lived as Aryans. We knew nothing of each other for a year and a half. It was very risky, for it was known that if someone was living with false documents, or in hiding, he was immediately shot.

In Germany, I was in the worst camp, Bergen-Belsen, from which not five percent came home alive.

I can only tell you that it is a miracle that I am here. If the Americans had not come, two days later, I could not have held out. I was so weak with hunger and hard work.

Thank God I found my wife and child in Budapest. They looked very ill. She had been five weeks with the child in a cellar during the front, without food; clothes and linens, she had exchanged for food. We have lost all we had, and we had some nice things.

The immigration cost us a lot. Thank God! We are here and happy. I came from the camp without a heller.[5] Good friends lent me money to send my wife and child to a health resort. During the time my family was away, I did business and earned some money, but it is unfortunately very little, we have nothing. Prices are very high. We must set up a home again, but we have no desire to remain here, where we have no friends. We should be glad to be with you. I would beg you to send us the affidavit [for immigration].

Unfortunately, I must inform you that I have no trace of Schalom and Pinchas and also other relations. My wife has lost her parents and brothers and sisters. One sister, who was deported in the year 1942, has come back, thank God! Otherwise we have no one left but you.

Our little child is now two-and-a-half years old, and pretty, but he knows nothing of chocolate and cocoa and other foods that we cannot get here. I would beg you, if convenient, to send him something. We are badly off for clothes; winter is coming on and it is hard to get anything here. I should be much obliged if you could send us some. I have a friend who has a daughter in Palestine. I have spoken to him and if you wish to send us money, kindly send to [name and address redacted]. The father of the girl would pay me here much more. When you send the money, kindly let me know.

How is dear Louisa and Sasi and Moischaleib? Please send us photos; my wife is longing to make your acquaintance.

I hope your wife and child are well.

Trusting to receive an early reply, and with hearty greetings and kisses,

Yours affectionately, David, Aranka and son Bandika

I'D FELT so very good thinking that the manuscript was finished, before I'd found this letter. However, I believe that my father was watching from above and saying, "Not so fast, Joe. This is my story, and here is a missing piece that I want included."

ACKNOWLEDGMENTS

WITH APPRECIATION to my parents, David and Aurelia Gold, for having the courage to pass on their stories of the Holocaust to and for the next generation.

I hope that this book has given special meaning and insight to my immediate family: Our loving children and our grandchildren, whom we ask to carry on the torch to the next generation.

THIS BOOK is also dedicated to: My dear brother Andy, who also survived the Holocaust. He is and has always been my role model and my best friend. Thank you for sharing all of your insights and first-hand memories of certain events in this book.

Yad Vashem in Jerusalem, for documentation from the archives and Shoah resource centre that has been graciously forwarded to my brother and me over a period of many years. Thank you also for the *Encyclopedia of Jewish Communities* and its information about the cities and towns of Slovakia. And to Wikipedia, for historical information on World War II events.

Thanks to Shira van den Berg, for the cover photograph; Laylie Woods, for assisting with the photos and documents used in the research and writing of this book; Marc Brooks, for assisting with the maps; and Alon Katsir, for assisting with the grammar and editing of this book. To Lucas van den Berg, Jason Woods, Lisa Brooks, and Adina Katsir for their moral support.

This book would not have been possible without the care, creativity, and talent of the Page Two team. To my editor, Amanda Lewis, thank you for the insight and editorial excellence you gave to shaping my family's story. To my copyeditor, Shyla Seller, and my proofreader, Alison Strobel, you helped breathe life into these words. To my book designer, Jennifer Lum, your artistry and eye for beauty captured the spirit of my parents' resilience and love. To my web developer and designer, Chris von Szombathy, your creativity and skill has helped us build a valuable online resource. To Jessica Werb, Lorraine Toor, and Deanna Roney, thank you for ensuring this book reaches audiences far and wide. Jesse Finkelstein, thank you for your supportive leadership and strategic guidance every step of the way. Caela Moffet, none of this would have come together without your oversight and attention to detail.

And finally, thank you to my wife, Karyn, for being my sounding board and cheerleader during this whole process. When the going got rough, you helped smooth out the bumps.

NOTES

1   A note on the maps and all place names throughout the book: many cities and towns found
themselves under the rule of different countries
and empires from the late 1800s until today. In
this book, I have used location names with
which the respective individual(s) associated
themselves.

2   Among others, US soldier Henry Kissinger
(later US statesman and Nobel laureate) was part
of the 84th Infantry Division of the US Army,
which liberated the Ahlem work camp on
April 10, 1945.

3   Bergen-Belsen is perhaps best known as the
death place of Anne and Margot Frank, who
both died of typhus there in February or March
1945, shortly before the camp was liberated.

4   While we were there in 1945, Hungary suffered
    the worst case of hyperinflation the world had
    ever seen. How bad was the inflation? Some-
    thing that cost 379 pengos in September 1944
    cost 72,330 pengos by January 1945; 453,886
    pengos by February; 1,872,910 pengos by
    March; 35,790,276 pengos by April; 11.267
    billion pengos by May 31; 862 billion pengos by
    June 15; 954 trillion pengos by June 30; 3 billion
    billion pengos by July 7; 11 trillion billion pengos
    by July 15, and 1 trillion trillion pengos by
    July 22, 1946. When we arrived in Budapest
    in 1942, the exchange rate was 5 pengos to the
    US dollar. Shortly after we left Hungary in 1945,
    it was 1.75 million pengos to the US dollar.

5   A German or Austrian coin of low value.

BIBLIOGRAPHY

American Friends of the Czech Republic. "The First World War and the Establishment of Czechoslovakia." https://afocr.org/first-world-war-and-establishment-czechoslovakia.

Ancestry. "Gross-Rosen Concentration Camp." Fold3 (database). https://www.fold3.com/page/286060914-gross-rosen-concentration-camp/stories.

Buchler, Yehoshua Robert, and Ruth Shachak (eds.). *Pinkas Hakehilot: Encyclopedia of Jewish Communities, Slovakia*. Jerusalem: Yad Vashem, 2003. https://www.jewishgen.org/yizkor/pinkas_slovakia/pinkas_Slovakia.html#TOC402.

Donin, Hayim H. *To Pray as a Jew: A Guide to the Prayer Book and the Synagogue Service*. New York: Basic Books, 1991.

Eisen, Max. *By Chance Alone: A Remarkable True Story of Courage and Survival at Auschwitz*. Toronto: HarperCollins Canada, 2016.

GlobalSecurity.org. "1933–1945: Krupp under the Nazis." https://www.globalsecurity.org/military/world/europe/krupp-08.htm.

Gold, David. *David G. Testimony 1984*. Videotaped interview with Dr. Robert Krell. Vancouver: Vancouver Holocaust Education Centre, 1984. https://collections.vhec.org/Detail/objects/1263.

Gutterman, Bella. *A Narrow Bridge to Life: Jewish Forced Labor and Survival in the Gross-Rosen Camp System, 1940–1945*. Oxford, NY: Berghahn Books, 2008.

Hellman, Peter. *The Auschwitz Album: A Book Based Upon an Album Discovered by a Concentration Camp Survivor, Lili Meier*. New York: Random House, 1981.

KZ-Gedenkstätte Neuengamme. "Hannover-Ahlem (A 12)." https://www.kz-gedenkstaette-neuen gamme.de/en/history/satellite-camps/satellite-camps/hannover-ahlem-a-12/.

———. "Hildesheim." https://www.kz-gedenk staette-neuengamme.de/en/history/satellite-camps/satellite-camps/hildesheim/.

Museum of the History of Polish Jews. "The Gross-Rosen Camp." Virtual Shtetl (database). https://sztetl.org.pl/en/towns/s/213-strzegom/116-sites-of-martyrdom/51159-gross-rosen-camp.

Museum of the Jewish People at Beit Hatfutsot. "Ricse." https://dbs.bh.org.il/place/ricse.

myCzechRepublic.com. "1918–1945: The First Republic and World War II." http://www.myczechrepublic.com/czech-history/first-republic.html.

National Committee for Attending Deportees. "The Holocaust in Hungary." http://degob.org/index.php?showarticle=2031.

Sambells, Chelsea. "Remembering Food in the Concentration Camps." *Chelsea Sambells* (blog), October 19, 2017. https://chelseasambells.com/2017/10/19/remembering-food-in-the-concentration-camps-interviews-with-holocaust-survivors/.

Schulweis, Rabbi Harold M. "Backwards and Forwards." In *Mahzor Lev Shalem for Rosh Hashanah and Yom Kippur*. New York: The Rabbinical Assembly, 2010.

Shurpin, Yehuda. "Why Do Jews Fly Their Dead to Israel for Burial?" Chabad.org. https://www.chabad.org/library/article_cdo/aid/3364937/jewish/Why-Do-Jews-Fly-Their-Dead-to-Israel-for-Burial.htm.

Steiner, F. (ed.). *The Tragedy of Slovak Jewry: Photographs and Documents*. Trans. F.O. Stein and J. Weiss. Bratislava, Czechoslovakia: Documentation Centre of CUJCR, 1949.

Taylor, Bryan. "The Worst Hyperinflations in History: Hungary," *Global Financial Data* (blog), April 16, 2014. http://globalfinancialdata.com/the-worst-hyperinflations-in-history-hungary/.

United States Holocaust Memorial Museum. "Bergen-Belsen: Key Dates." In *Holocaust Encyclopedia*. Washington: United States Holocaust Memorial Museum. https://encyclopedia.ushmm.org/content/en/article/bergen-belsen.

———. "Bergen-Belsen in Depth: The Camp Complex." In *Holocaust Encyclopedia*. Washington: United States Holocaust Memorial Museum. https://encyclopedia.ushmm.org/content/en/article/bergen-belsen-in-depth-the-camp-complex.

Weiner Holocaust Library. "How Did Survivors Rebuild their Lives?" The Holocaust Explained. https://www.theholocaustexplained.org/survival-and-legacy/rebuilding-lives-case-studies/.

Wikipedia, The Free Encyclopedia. "Arrow Cross Party." https://en.wikipedia.org/wiki/Arrow_Cross_Party.

———. "Bergen-Belsen Concentration Camp." https://en.wikipedia.org/wiki/Bergen-Belsen_concentration_camp.

———. "Bombing of Hanover in World War II." https://en.wikipedia.org/wiki/Bombing_of_Hanover_in_World_War_II.

———. "History of the Jews in Hungary." https://en.wikipedia.org/wiki/History_of_the_Jews_in_Hungary.

———. "The Holocaust in Slovakia." https://en.wikipedia.org/wiki/The_Holocaust_in_Slovakia.

———. "Kisvárda." https://en.wikipedia.org/wiki/Kisvárda.

———. "Manfréd Weiss Steel and Metal Works." https://en.wikipedia.org/wiki/Manfréd_Weiss_Steel_and_Metal_Works.

———. "Modeh Ani." https://en.wikipedia.org/wiki/Modeh_Ani.

———. "Project Riese." https://en.wikipedia.org/wiki/Project_Riese.

———. "Shmuel Dovid Unger." https://en.wikipedia.org/wiki/Shmuel_Dovid_Ungar.

———. "Siege of Budapest." https://en.wikipedia.org/wiki/Siege_of_Budapest.

Yad Vashem. "Historical Background: The Jews of Hungary during the Holocaust" (article). https://www.yadvashem.org/articles/general/jews-of-hungary-during-the-holocaust.html.

———. *The Story of the Jewish Community in Bratislava* (exhibition). https://www.yadvashem.org/yv/en/exhibitions/communities/bratislava/index.asp.

———. "The World of the Camps." The Holocaust (series of articles). https://www.yadvashem.org/holocaust/about/camps.html.

INDEX

ABOUT THE AUTHOR

 JOE GOLD was born in Czecho-slovakia in 1947 and immigrated to Vancouver, Canada, in 1948. He attended the University of British Columbia and worked in the family textile business, followed by a career in real estate development, management, and software. He played keyboards in an R&B band, and loves life, family, sports, and music. Joe is married with nine grandchildren.